Information Design
Desk Reference

...Upon this gifted age, in its dark hour
Falls from the sky a meteoric shower
Of facts...they lie unquestioned, uncombined.
Wisdom enough to leech us of our ill
Is daily spun; but there exists no loom
To weave it into fabric...

Sonnet from **Huntsman, What Quarry?**
by Edna St. Vincent Millay

Information Design
Desk Reference

Christine Sevilla

Menlo Park, California

Information Design Desk Reference
Christine Sevilla

© **2002 Crisp Publications, Inc.**
Printed in the United States of America by Von Hoffmann Graphics, Inc.

Credits:
Editor: George Young
Design & Production: lumin guild
Production Manager: Judy Petry

CrispLearning.com
01 02 03 04 10 9 8 7 6 5 4 3 2 1
LCCN 2001088396
Sevilla, Christine
Information Design Desk Reference
ISBN 1-56052-610-6

Table of Contents

Content control
Basic design
Page design
Color
Document appearance
Incorporating graphic elements
The variety of documents
Presentation media
Web sites

Introduction   1

Content Control   5
       know your audience   7
       how people learn   11
       objectives   19
       organizing information   23
       clarifying information   27

Basic Design   37
    design and visual logic   39
    elements of design   41
    principles of design   45

Page Design   51
    elements of page design   53
    manipulating text blocks   61
    style-setting   67
    emphasis with text   69
    direct the reader's eye   71
    developing your layout   75
    graphic placement   79
    typeface and fonts   83
    type and legibility   89

Color   91
    color basics   93
    popular connotations of colors   101
    color in information design   105

Document Appearance   107
    paper   109
    stationery   113
    document sequence   121
    covers   127
    binding   129

Incorporating Graphic Elements   133
    when to use a graphic   135
    photo or illustration?   137
    the power of graphics   141
    making your graphic communicate   143
    tables   145
    charts and graphs   149
    diagrams   161

The Variety of Documents   165
       brochures   167
       postcards   175
       newsletters   177
       spreadsheets   185
       reports and manuals   191
       forms   199
       posters   211
       wall charts   217
       job aids   219
       résumés   223

Presentation Media   231
       presentation media overview   233
       overheads   243
       slides   249
       presentation software   253
       video   259
       flipcharts   263

Web Sites   267
       user viewpoint   269
       using the Web effectively   291

Glossary   299

Reference List   307

Index   311

Project Table of Contents

Any project
Conference
Financial document or budget
Intra-office communication
Job aid or procedure
Newsletter
Office image/identity
Presentation
Report, proposal, or manual
Web site

Any project

know your audience	7
how people learn	11
objectives	19
organizing information	23
clarifying information	27
elements of page design	53
manipulating text blocks	61
style-setting	67
emphasis with text	69
direct the reader's eye	71
developing your layout	75

graphic placement 79
typeface and fonts 83
type and legibility 89

Conference

color basics 93
color in information design 105
making your graphic communicate 143
brochures 167
reports and manuals 191
forms 199
posters 211

Financial document or budget

making your graphic communicate 143
tables 145
charts and graphs 149
spreadsheets 185

Intra-office communication

when to use a graphic 135
photo or illustration? 137
the power of graphics 141
making your graphic communicate 143
newsletters 177
reports and manuals 191
forms 199
wall charts 217

Job aid or procedure

color basics 93
popular connotations of color 101
color in information design 105
making your graphic communicate 143
tables 145
charts and graphs 149
diagrams 161

posters   211
wall charts   217
job aids   219

Newsletter

color basics   93
popular connotations of color   101
color in information design   105
paper   109
when to use a graphic   135
photo or illustration?   137
the power of graphics   141
making your graphic communicate   143
newsletters   177

Office image/identity

color basics   93
popular connotations of color   101
color in information design   105
paper   109
stationery   113
covers   127
binding   129
brochures   167
postcards   175

Presentation

color basics   93
popular connotations of color   101
color in information design   105
when to use a graphic   135
photo or illustration?   137
the power of graphics   141
making your graphic communicate   143
presentation media overview   233
overheads   243
slides   249

presentation software   253
video   259
flipcharts   263

Report, proposal, or manual
color basics   93
popular connotations of color   101
color in information design   105
paper   109
document sequence   121
covers   127
binding   129
when to use a graphic   135
photo or illustration?   137
the power of graphics   141
making your graphic communicate   143
tables   145
charts and graphs   149
diagrams   161

Web site
color basics   93
popular connotations of color   101
color in information design   105
when to use a graphic   135
photo or illustration?   137
the power of graphics   141
making your graphic communicate   143
brochures   167
user viewpoint   269
using the Web effectively   291

Preface

I've looked long and hard for a resource that ordinary humans can use when they need to produce a document, simple brochure, poster, presentation or anything else they might need to combine text and graphics in meaningful ways. In my instructional design work, I must be conscious of how information is presented and how that presentation promotes learning. I have found useful resources, but they were often aimed at graphic designers or people who did considerable amounts of what has been called desktop publishing.

Most of us need to be able to produce a presentation or business letter that has the appropriate impact but does not cost us significant time in preparation or learning curve. So I started to create my own reference, which grew into this book and would have kept growing had my publisher not given me a deadline. If I'd had the time, I would have included many more illustrations, and a forklift would be a required accessory for readers. Keeping this a quick reference meant keeping the weight down.

There are people to thank:
My husband, Timothy Wells, for his support and infinite patience during the months of work on this book.

My father, Michael Sevilla, for encouraging me to explore designing everything from jewelry to clothing.

My dear friend, Milton Lederman, Ph.D., for his kind, red-pen review to rid this book entirely of all punctuation errors, except for those I added after his edit—just to assure readers I'm human, of course.

Introduction

Information design is about communication that makes the complex clear. It is often described as the effort to organize the patterns in data to create meaningful information and a path to understanding. The focus is the user's response. Information needs to be organized, easy to find, and sequenced appropriately to achieve the order that will help a reader or viewer to navigate a written work or presentation. Good design is both esthetic and functional; it should be capable of evoking a positive response and at the same time serve its purpose well. By supporting successful communication, good design makes us more efficient.

I offer this book as a reference for business people, knowledge workers, anyone who must present information clearly. That is why there are two points of entry into the book: a standard table of contents and a project table of contents, describing what you might want to review if you are creating a brochure, for example.

The pages of the book have large margins, for illustrations and for you to add your own notes. In keeping with my instructional habit, I've added a few activities—the gray boxes—for the reader who wishes to get some relevant practice.

I decided to use a basic word processing application for this entire book to show the casual user that he or she does not need to be an expert at one of the publishing programs to come up with a good product. All but one of the examples were created using standard software that comes with every personal computer; no complex drawing packages or specialty applications were used. The publisher merely took my file and used it "as is" since I typed every word and created every graphic—only the cover was designed and produced by the publisher. So, if the illustrations and graphics look like something you could do, you are right!

There are two consistent, but brief, rants you'll find throughout the book. I argue for white space. Give the viewer's eyes a rest. And I argue for simplicity. When designing, it's easier to handle fewer elements in a document or presentation, certainly. More importantly, we humans are symbol manipulators; draw attention to too many elements and our viewers can't decipher the true message.

Even if you are new at this, you know what you like. Start by collecting samples of what works for you: brochures, flyers, annual reports or even addresses for Web sites that you find eye-catching and informative. By collecting samples you can begin to train your eye. Begin to ask yourself what patterns, contrasts and formats are attractive to you. You will be on your way to developing your own style.

Content Control

My struggle has been to discover the road, the pattern that leads to memory.
The junctures of road-to-road and path-to-path celebrate that connection. That
connection is learning, and learning is remembering what you are interested in.
Richard Saul Wurman

know your audience

The first thing anyone creating a document, a Web site, or any other communication should do is perform an analysis of the target audience. Take the time to really consider the people you want to reach. Who are they? What will be the most effective way to reach them? Consider hobbies, lifestyles, tastes, goals, values, psychological traits—anything that can help you match the material to the audience. Hobbies, you ask? Well, perhaps you know that they're all sports fans: you can use examples from football plays to illustrate and enhance your points. They will understand more and enjoy the process, too.

analyzing a target audience

Use this checklist, adapted from Robert F. Mager's *Making Instruction Work*, to ensure that you are meeting your customer's needs with whatever you are creating. If there are big holes in your knowledge, get out there and talk to a few people who seem to fit the basic description of "target audience members." Or, do some library research. You can find every kind of interesting statistic in the library that will help you to ensure that your message is focused on its intended recipient.

Mager's common sense little "formula" for creating instruction, based on this analysis, gives you the best possible starting point. You might not be creating instruction, but no matter what you are creating, you certainly don't want to hear them snoring right away! Here is Mager's formula:

What they need to be able to do
- **What they can already do**
   The instruction

That's a big part of analyzing your audience. You want to start your instruction, as much as possible, just at the point where their knowledge stops. Of course, most audiences are diverse. But how diverse? And just what are their overall characteristics? Listing the attributes of your audience, and thinking about things from the audience's perspective, will help you to design something they will find useful.

the checklist

To develop your target audience analysis, consider the questions below, adapted from Mager, and follow up on the items most important for your work.

needs
— Why do they need the information you provide?

— How will they use the information you provide?

— What rewards will result from their use of the information you provide?

expertise
— How much do they already know?

— Are they knowledgeable about the subject?

— Are they novices?

demographics
— Is the group predominately male or female, or is the mix equal?

— What are their ages? Are their ages similar?

— Will there be language barriers?

— What ethnic backgrounds must be considered?

— Do they assimilate information similarly?

work considerations
— What fields do they work in?

— What organizations do they work in?

— What are their occupations: are they in executive, technical, or specialist positions?

— Are they reading, reviewing, participating because they want to or because they've been required to do so?

— How much time do they have to devote to your material?

— Do they have the required resources to use what you are providing?

— Will they be able to take the time to use what you are providing?

education
— How well do they read (or do math…consider any entering ability important to your creation)?

— What are their educational backgrounds?

— Is there significant variation within the group?

interests
— What are their interests?

— What are their tastes?

— What hobbies do they participate in?

social and psychological factors

— Where will they be (describe the environment) when receiving the information you provide?

— What lifestyle characteristics would you expect them to exhibit?

— What are their goals?

— What do they value?

— What do they find rewarding?

— What attitudes can be anticipated?

— What are their hot-buttons: what words, images, data should be stressed or avoided?

— Do they possess significant psychological traits?

how people learn

Am I kidding? Cover how people learn in one short chapter? Not possible, I know. But we can all use an introduction to some of the thought on the subject because of the perspective it offers on the presentation of information.

Robert M. Gagné described nine "instructional events," and I think anyone presenting information they hope others will understand can benefit from reviewing his thoughts on the process. Certainly you want to start by (**1**) igniting interest and (**2**) telling them what they can expect to learn. Then you'll (**3**) tell them how the subject relates to something they know. Gagné, and others who came after him, had a lot to say about (**4**) presenting content. It depends on the type of learning that needs to be done. What? Yes, now we'll see how he classified learning in order to support and enhance the learning process. If you're interested in knowing more about the remaining events in the list shown here, look at Gagné's work or an instructional design text.

Gagné's instructional events

1. Gain attention
2. Tell them what they'll learn
3. Recall prior learning
4. Present the content
5. Provide guidance
6. Elicit performance
7. Provide feedback
8. Assess performance
9. Enhance retention/transfer

All the authorities on how people learn classify types of learning, and there are many good schema to choose from. Gagné's learning classification is still most useful. He said that classifying the performance to be learned helps to guide designing instruction for that performance. The scheme forms the basis for strategies to help people to learn what is presented to them. The way you present a topic or concept will define how your audience absorbs it.

Gagné's learning classification, simplified

Cognitive	**Verbal information**
	What is known and enables further learning. Often, information dissemination is the only goal for your presentation or report. Certainly much of our education system is based on imparting information and requiring students to restate it.
	Intellectual skills:
	Information is manipulated with intellectual skills. In general, providing examples is essential.
	<u>Discrimination:</u> Distinguishing one thing from another and deciding if it is the *same or different*. How does an advertiser help customers to discriminate between two brands?
	<u>Concepts:</u> *Identifying a class of objects or definitions.* For example, pointing out all of the electronic devices on your desk would be evidence of identifying a concrete concept. Concepts can be defined, too. If you can locate all the misplaced modifiers in a group of sentences, you have demonstrated that you can identify a defined concept.
	<u>Rules:</u> "Rules make it possible for us to respond to a class of things with a *class of performances*." Gagné says it well; examples help. You've undoubtedly attempted to diagram a sentence or fill out a form. You were following some prescribed procedures. You are engaging in a higher order form of rule when solving a problem new to you.

Attitude	Attitudes affect our behaviors and the choices we make. For example, the video created by United Way each year for distribution to employees tugs on the heartstrings—the goal is to change attitudes through an emotional appeal.
Cognitive combined with Attitude	Cognitive strategies, according to Gagné, are the ways we manage our learning and thinking. You organize your office for peak efficiency. You map the shortest route to work. We can't see the cognitive strategy; we have to infer it from what we see. As I've been called upon to observe people doing their work, I have asked them to please narrate so that I can understand why they are doing what they are doing, their cognitive strategy.
Motor	Motor skills make many of our performances possible, from brushing our hair to running a race.

You're still with me? It looks as if we took a detour. Nope. Now, we're going to look at what kinds of approaches to employ for the items in the intellectual learning category.

delivery strategies

What are the best delivery strategies? Here are a few pearls of wisdom to help you design an effective presentation of your subject matter, based on the good work of Timothy J. Newby and Donald A. Stepich in their article, "Designing Instruction: Practical Strategies."

Information: Most important to imparting information is giving your audience tools by which to remember it. Give them a way to code it mentally for later retrieval. Some examples include:

— Analogy   liken it to something they know

— Story   put it in a context they can relate to

— Activity   give them an exercise that requires recall or allows them to devise their own cues

— Mnemonic	create a word from a series of letters, such as ASAP for "as soon as possible"
— Format	group like items, arrange items in an outline, or make some items larger or bolder for emphasis

Discrimination: Ways to help people to recognize the difference between one thing and another:

— Discuss only one item at a time.

— Simplify the item to reduce distraction.

— Emphasize distinguishing features.

— Perhaps you are demonstrating bird songs. Can the audience discriminate between the mockingbird's mimicry and the song of a bird mimicked by the mockingbird?

Concepts: Concepts can be concrete or defined. In general, the following steps apply:

1   Give the concept a label.

2   Present a best example of the concept and mention key features.

3   Next, present examples and non-examples, beginning with examples that possess all of the relevant characteristics then ending with the range of examples possessing fewer of the relevant characteristics. Or present divergent pairs and gradually reduce the differences between pairs presented. The non-examples chosen can make or break the learning. To be sure your audience doesn't get distracted by irrelevant characteristics, don't start with non-examples that are wildly different from the examples.

4   Finally, randomly present the concept on its own. Allow people to identify it and be sure they really "get it."

To bring this to life a bit, I put together some video segments with employees acting out breaches of confidentiality, or situations that seem like breaches of confidentiality, in the health care setting. At the beginning of the training program, after confidentiality was defined, the segments were shown in a sequence starting with the obvious breaches, to the more subtle breaches of confidentiality, to situations that are not examples of breaches of confidentiality. Then, the trainees were given additional scenarios to classify as examples or non-examples of breaches.

Rules: We are doing something when we use rules. Rules allow us to combine concepts or symbols in specific relationships for a purpose, with a new result. Important to rule using is identifying the cues from the environment that prompt rule-using behavior.

— Begin with the end in mind. For example, telling people to solve for X indicates exactly what they should end up with—a value for X.

— Describe and sequence the concepts that make up the rule as needed. In diagramming a sentence, you need to identify nouns, verbs, objects, and so on to show their relationships within a sentence.

— Give people a chance to practice applying the rule in a safe situation, then in increasingly novel situations.

We humans use rules constantly. Let's say you have a new employee who will be stocking new arrivals on the shelves in your bookstore. The goal is to place stock in the appropriate locations, on the shelves or in a holding area for special orders. He needs to know the procedures and decisions for placing books in different locations. You'll have to show him the places to look on the books' covers for their categories, and you'll map out the location of categories in the store. There won't be a one-to-one correspondence, so he'll need some other decision rules. He'll get going by observing the layout and operations of the store, observing other employees in action, being observed while doing the simple stuff and getting feedback, and finally, by gradually taking on the more complicated stocking tasks.

more about adult learning

Learning styles and preferences are also important to promoting learning, or presenting information for understanding. We have all done the magazine survey to assess whether we are primarily visual, auditory, or kinesthetic learners. What is important is finding a way to reach the variety of learning styles by presenting information in different ways. That doesn't mean you create multiple presentations for every point you plan to make, although repetition is important to ensuring that learning takes place. The three groupings of learning styles mentioned above play an important role in retaining new knowledge, but there are other factors we could consider.

Susan Rundle of Performance Concepts International has participated in development of an excellent assessment tool, called the Building Excellence Inventory (BE for short), for defining an array of elements that determine how we process, internalize, and retain new information. The tool provides far more than a list of attributes. Instead, results are presented along a continuum. It's valuable to see all the different dimensions affecting learning and performance that this assessment measures. I'll describe the two dimensions that influence decisions in presenting information:

Perceptual elements: The perceptual elements described by the BE cover much more than auditory, visual, and kinesthetic. Visual is further divided into Visual Pictures and Visual Words. People with a strong preference for Visual Words tend to remember what they read very well while those with a strong preference for Visual Pictures are better able to retain information presented graphically. If you're explaining the tight standard deviation of scores on your customer-satisfaction survey, you would be well advised to show it graphically and to describe it in words. The repetition will help both the Visual Pictures and Visual Words learners, and they will focus in on the presentation style that engages them.

Other continua include Tactual, Internal Kinesthetic, External Kinesthetic. You can guess what the highly Tactual types are like: they like to fidget, perhaps by writing or doodling, or they need some concurrent physical expression, like tapping a pen. A highly External Kinesthetic person likes to get physically involved with the task while a highly Internal Kinesthetic person likes a personal or emotional involvement with the task.

Marketers, news media, and, frankly, lots of disciplines take advantage of these perceptual elements. Companies frequently send us samples of products. I often receive promotional items, such as pens with soft grips, that marketers hope I will find irresistible. Emotional appeals are a compelling way to move people to action. News stories are often written from the perspective of one person bravely fighting adversity. Presenting the emotional dimension must be done carefully, but it can lead to heightened interest and action.

Psychological elements: One important continuum covers the range from Global to Analytic. These dimensions describe how we process information. While I knew I was a "big picture person," I learned, for example, that I am very strongly Global, as opposed to Analytic. The world is better prepared for Analytics, who prefer detail, usually in a linear sequence that builds to the overall concept. I drive Analytics crazy because I can start a project in the middle and often create a step-by-step outline only when I'm well into it. I'm not doing things wrong, just differently. I still get the work done.

As an intensely Global type, I can't stand the many Web sites that have a home page stuffed with undifferentiated links, boxes of different content and tiny writing of every description. In keeping with my Global preference, my own Web site has a very simple home page, with links to four different types of information. I'll admit that a site with lots of links and content on the home page can work as long as it is organized well with a good layout.

The psychological elements also include a Reflective/Impulsive continuum. Let's say you are writing a critical safety procedure for employees in a nuclear reactor. It would be important to consider how to prevent the Impulsive types from jumping to action too quickly (does anyone hire Impulsive types for work in nuclear reactors?). Give them useful tasks to perform, tasks that clarify the situation, before the action can be taken. Similarly, if you are writing a biohazard procedure, you don't want people to reflect too long on whether or not to seek first aid. Give them a time frame.

The other elements: The BE is different because it measures twenty different preferences, ranging from mobility, time of day, internal motivation, and interest in working with groups to a number of other factors. This is the first tool I have seen that accounts for the effect of different environmental preferences for light, temperature, setting, and sound on learning and performance. When you consider your target audience for your information, you should consider their setting and how it will influence receipt of your message.

You can't predict what your audience's preferences will be, but you can design information with, for example, enough visual support to aid those who need the spatial view, in addition to a complete verbal description. In my instructional design work, I try to give people as many options as possible. In an online course, I provide a paper booklet and texts for the Tactual people; this serves also for the people who like a less formal setting (say on a couch, rather than at a desk) for reading. In that same online course, people have a variety of activities, including discussion, research, writing, and group collabo-ration. Some activities require interaction, with the emotional component that can be so compelling, while other components are more solitary, providing time for reflection and a chance for knowl-edge to "sink in." I present a high-level structure for the course in the syllabus, but it's in outline form so that the Analytical folks can see the detail they crave.

Understanding your own learning and performance preferences will help you to find the fastest path to absorbing new information or to performing work most productively. Understanding the array of dimensions affecting the human capacity for processing information will sharpen your ability to present information most effectively.

objectives

This will sound familiar. You can't write or develop anything without knowing what you want to achieve or accomplish. Do you want people to learn how to do something, or do you want them to request your services in the future? If you teach them something useful you just might interest them in your services as a result. So, start with what you want as an outcome and build your content around that desired outcome.

If you want them to learn something from your book, Web site, presentation, or whatever your are creating, it helps to have some background in building objectives a la Robert Mager, the instructional design guru. Why? They will form a solid basis for your work and help you organize it before you fill in the content. Good objectives will force you to create better and more organized content.

In instruction, learning objectives are measurable statements of the intended outcomes from a training or education course. They describe what you want people to be able to do after they finish the course or session. Objectives provide the guidelines to frame what needs to be taught, and they provide summary statements to help you to arrange the sequence of the items to be presented in an appropri-

ate order. Development of any document or presentation can benefit from well-crafted objectives. If you intend to convey a message,
list a few objectives.

In training, objectives describe a trainee's performance, the conditions under which the performance occurs, and the standard of
acceptable performance. The breakdown, according to Robert F.
Mager again, is like this:

performance	what someone should be able to do—in specific and action-oriented language
condition	circumstances in which the doing will occur
criteria	how to tell or measure when the performance is good enough.

Some examples:

Condition- Performance- Criteria-	Given an interface specification, the student will be able to write a Java script, which will display information identically in the two major browsers.
Condition- Performance- Criteria-	Given a fully equipped kitchen and ingredients, the learner will be able to make a cream sauce that does not separate or curdle.
Condition- Performance- Criteria-	After my presentation, the committee will be able to adjust its budget to within 5% of the new target.

They have some similarities. Each states a performance—what the
person should be able to do. Each gives a condition, as in given a
"specification" or a "fully equipped kitchen." Each gives an idea of
the criteria for performance, or how well it needs to be done—

"display information identically in two browsers" or "does not separate or curdle."

Notice that I said descriptors of performance should be ACTION words? Look at the two sets of verbs below and choose the set you think works to create a strong performance objective.

know	**describe**
understand	**identify**
appreciate	**build**
grasp	**recite**
value	**write**

If you agree with me, you chose the verbs on the right. Instructors want to create objectives that describe an action that is observable. It is impossible to observe whether or not someone values, grasps, appreciates, understands, or knows anything.

But you might not be as concerned with motivating actual behaviors. Perhaps you simply need to provide your audience with awareness of a topic, or you are giving a keynote address. Then, verbs like "appreciate" can be used in that case, and you can forget about conditions and criteria. I don't use the weaker verbs because building strong behavioral objectives is a habit with me. I tend to build training and instruction meant to change behavior, and I rarely give a presentation where I don't want the audience to take something away they can really act upon.

Try to write an objective for some work you are about to begin, or simply write one for baking a cake or planting a tree. Use the format—performance/condition/criteria—as a guide if your objective describes a behavior, as baking a cake does. Ignore the condition and criteria if you don't expect any performance to follow from your presentation, document...whatever you are creating.

organizing information

You choose the way you organize your information by the way you want it to be found. Richard Saul Wurman, in his book *Information Architects*, has defined five ways to organize information, LATCH for short:

L **Location**
A **Alphabet**
T **Time**
C **Category**
H **Hierarchy**

location

Examples include a site map in a Web site, or a road map, or a diagram of a library, showing the history section, art section, and so on. Think of a good example of a building map that gives you a good sense of where you are in relation to your destination. Or, think of a bad example: you arrive in the lobby of a 20-story building and you know the name of the business you want to visit, but the listing is by floor. You have to read the list for every floor to find your destination.

alphabet

The dictionary, any encyclopedia, a glossary all are organized alphabetically because their numerous entries all have approximately equal importance. The alphabetic organization of information is misused frequently. Be careful not to bury important information among items of lesser importance by alphabetizing.

time

Schedules and calendars and project plans are organized by time. There are some beautiful examples of history timelines on the Web, particularly on the PBS site, where more information about a period can be obtained with a click from a clear, simple illustration. I took a picture of one beautiful example of a train schedule during a visit to Kyoto, Japan.

奈良線時刻表
Nara Line Departure Time

宇治・奈良方面
for Uji, Nara

毎日

5	35₁₀				
6	6₁₀	49₁₀			
7	15₁₀	49₁₀	54₁₀		
8	9₁₀	24₁₀	38₁₀	57₁₀	
9	11₁₀	26₁₀	38₁₀	51₁₀	57₁₀
10	17₁₀	40₁₀	51₁₀	57₁₀	
11	17₁₀	40₁₀	51₁₀	57₁₀	

Only critical elements appear in the chart

Only essential, unique data are recorded. The first digit of the hour appears down the left side with last two digits shown to the right. Track number is shown in small type next to the time. It becomes a very descriptive graphic, viewed in its entirety. Note the pattern of the train departure times—many more at peak hour, like a bar chart. This presentation makes it easy to glance at the most pertinent information and to drill down quickly to supporting information.

category

Topics or content of similar importance can be organized into categories. For example, if you're looking for something in the yellow page section of your phone book, with any luck you know how the item you are looking for is categorized, or you might need to use the index to the yellow pages. If you are creating categories for a document or an illustration, use the most commonly accepted vocabulary and combine items that logically belong together when grouping information. You don't want to make your readers or viewers work too hard, so consider why they are interested in your message.

ACME Departments	
Service	555-1000
Sales	555-2000
Parts	555-3000

hierarchy

Think of hierarchy as an organization by continuum from biggest to smallest, most important to least important, most expensive to least expensive, and so on. Often, it is convenient to assign numbers or values to orders of magnitude, as is done in an outline. An organization chart is an obvious example of a hierarchy. With luck, the links within a Web site provide a predictable hierarchy of information.

The example of some language groupings from most to least specific, with one group (Latin languages) broken out for more detail, is another good example of a hierarchy. Keep in mind that the hierarchy only makes sense when the categories or groupings are meaningful to the reader.

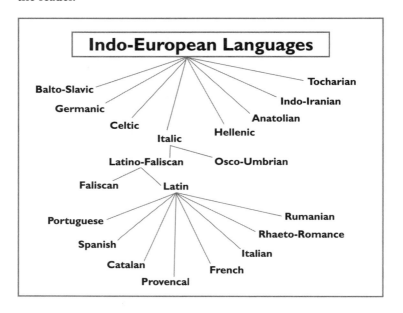

clarifying information

Your goal with whatever you are writing or developing is to provide a clear path to understanding. There are many ways to do it, depending upon the circumstances.

write extremely well

Yes, it takes practice, and feedback, and practicing some more. There are strategies you can employ, like defining the overall goal, for example. How will your reader (or viewer) respond, and what do you want your reader to come away with? Ask constantly if each element contributes to your goal. An outline of the skeleton of what you want to say can then be created. You can fill in the outline (or mind map or whatever helps you think it through) with detailed content. Seeing the big picture, or outline, first will help you to take the content to the right conclusion. I'm not saying there is only one linear way to write (goal→outline→fill in outline, etc.). I could never write that way myself. I am saying that you have to see the endpoint before you start. If filling in content in the middle section first works for you, do it.

The same rules apply to writing as to many other endeavors. It takes planning and careful execution. A separate editorial reviewer is critical, particularly if that editor knows the intended audience for your work. Get a target audience member to review your work and give you her reaction. Then, have the best writer you know go over it. What is the reaction? Have you oversimplified? Or, did you get lost in a deep tangent? Oversimplification will put your audience to sleep or it may even insult them. They want the most meaning and learning you can pack into a small space. Tangents will simply lose them.

Organizing written content also includes editing for clarity and appropriateness. The goal, content, and the audience will dictate how you approach each effort. Usually crisp, concise sentences will drive a point in a business presentation. I know a really fine editor, David Creelman, Knowledge Manager at HR.com. Here's his take on editing: "The key thing I do is attempt to shorten sentences. This is actually my main editing trick…I always ask if I can take out a clause, a phrase and 'or x' or an 'and y' without ruining the sentence. As long as it doesn't ruin the sentence, then I go ahead."

Yes—the kind of editing we don't see often enough is editing for brevity. Enough said about that!

There is an exception to all this talk of crisp and concise. In an emotional request, say for funding, some metaphorical language and story telling would be in order. But this takes skill. Done badly, it's putrid. If you must tug on heartstrings or make an emotional pitch, be careful. Get an editor's help.

Finding an editor willing to help shouldn't be hard. Ask people in the public relations or communications department of your organization for the name of a good editor. Or call a local news publication and ask for a recommendation.

keep it readable

Your document must be readable. The *Xerox Publishing Standards* includes a description of the Kernel distance theory, a test of readability that defines the kernel of a sentence as the noun and the verb.

According to the theory, the greater the distance between noun and verb, the harder the sentence is to read. Similarly, modifiers that appear distant from the words they modify can convey unintended meaning. An example from the *Harbrace College Handbook* illustrates the point: "Newspapers carried the story of the quarterback's fumbling all over the country."

The *Standards* also includes a description of one of the readability scales, developed by Edward Fry. Many word processing applications have a built-in readability test to analyze sentence structure, sentence length, and word difficulty. If you write for a general audience, get into the habit of checking documents that you write with these tests. If you can keep your writing level at eighth grade, about 85 percent of the adult population will be able to read it.

I've compiled the laundry list you see here to help you identify weak writing. These very useful principles of writing are a subset of those listed on page 3-3 of *Xerox Publishing Standards*. I've added several, too.

— **Write about subject matter you know well.** I could try to write about astrophysics, but I wouldn't fool anyone.

— **Write in an informal, conversational style.** You've read pieces by people who can write just the way they talk, and it's as though you can hear them. It's more engaging because you feel the writer is talking with you, not at you.

— **Put people into your writing.** That's not always easy to do. Journalists do it all the time! They grab you by starting an article with a story about the old woman who lives in a shoe! Pulls you right in! Pick up a newspaper or newsmagazine and see which items are most compelling.

— **Keep paragraphs short.** One main idea per paragraph is plenty.

— **Keep most sentences short and simple.** Do vary the length and complexity of sentences, but keep them lean overall. Long, complex, or wordy sentences distract the reader, possibly into leaving your presentation entirely.

— **Write in active voice.** Passive voice is harder to understand and very stiff and formal sounding. Here's an example of passive voice: "Evil ways will be renounced by the candidate." Wouldn't it be better to say it straight? "The candidate promises to change his evil ways." If you are using a verb like "be" or "is" frequently, it's likely you need to do some rewriting.

— **Get to the point.** Don't drive readers crazy unraveling your meaning. Faulkner got away with complexity, but most of the rest of us don't do it so well! Instead of, "The Board had an unfavorable reaction to the plan, overall," try "The Board disliked the plan."

— **Pronouns must agree in gender.** It's common to see, and hear, sentences like, "When one works hard, they get rewarded." I have read that this usage is becoming acceptable. I say no. You can be clearer. The English language does pose some challenges, but you can figure out a way to overcome them. I switch gender with each use of the pronoun he/she. So, the sentence could read, "When one works hard, she gets rewarded." In this case, ignoring the gender pronouns as in, "Hard work is rewarded," which, while passive, would be the best solution.

— **Pronoun antecedents must be clear.** For instance, "John told William he had made a mistake." Who made the mistake?

— **Keep the modifier close to the word modified.** What I mean is, put the modifying word next to the word it describes. Here's some lovely imagery from my favorite grammar text, *Harbrace College Handbook:* "Having a broken arm and nose, I thought the statue was very ugly."

— **Use parallel construction.** "In January, February or in March" is sloppy. "In January, in February, or in March" is expressed consistently. So is "In January, February, or March."

— **Eliminate clichés.** Now yer talkin'.

— **Omit useless words.** Every word must support the message. Get rid of phrases like "in terms of" or "for the purpose of" and "at the present time" or, my pet peeve, "with regard to." Be ruthless when editing your work. Sharpen up every sentence.

— **Use simple, concrete, familiar words** rather than technical or abstract words, unless you're writing about a technical or abstract subject.

— **Use acronyms and abbreviations sparingly.** Even if you explain them with the first use, you can lose your audience if your document looks like alphabet soup.

— **Rewrite,** rewrite, rewrite. Get an editor to help you if you can't do it yourself.

Writing well takes practice and some help from experts. Take a writing class. Have others read your drafts to help you identify your most frequent writing problems. Pay an editor who comes highly recommended or ask a writer to recommend one. Read a classic like William Zinsser's *On Writing Well*—a quick read and full of tips for the new writer. Pick up a style guide from one of the leading newspapers. Get an excellent reference work, such as the Strunk and White classic, *The Elements of Style,* and keep a grammar guide handy. I love the *Harbrace College Handbook* I had to buy as a freshman in college. Not only does if offer great advice, but I keep a bookmark in the misplaced modifiers section in case I need a giggle. (Just for fun, here's an example: "After eating our lunch, the bus departed.")

plan ahead

Seems obvious, doesn't it? As an instructor, I've seen enough hasty reports to know that procrastination is universal. I promise that if you don't procrastinate you will have a much better outcome! I always write as soon as I can when I have an assignment to complete. Then I review it a few days later. It is amazing what you can miss when you are in the middle of it all. Planning ahead includes gathering the essentials, sequencing them, outlining, and even creating a storyboard, depending upon the assignment. Storyboards are described in the chapter on presentation media.

relate new items to things known

This is similar to that except for:
X -------
Y -------
Z -------

Remember that fellow named Robert M. Gagné, who defined the steps in the process of teaching a subject new to the learner? After you get the learner's attention, the next item on the agenda is to recall prior learning. I liken prior learning to a framework upon which to hang the new stuff. Suppose you want to tell a group something about how your city's new transit system will function. Suppose further that they know about the Metro in DC or BART in the Bay Area, so you can mention those and begin to describe differences and perhaps a few key similarities to reassure them. That's all you need to tell them.

Here's a story for you: I was once treated to a meeting about management reports from the new information system. The person who was to lead the meeting entered carrying a multi-foot-high stack of reports. Then she distributed the four-inch thick packets out of the stack and began to go over the first report, field by field, in exhaustive detail. After a polite period we asked if she could summarize the differences between current and new reports. It would have taken some preparation, but a quick guide to differences in key reports would have saved us all a bit of time and spared the meeting leader's reputation.

use symbols

A few situations lend themselves perfectly to symbols or icons. Many situations do not. An example of a good use of symbol—a book on flowering plants that includes simple symbols for shade or sun, perennial or annual, dry or wet conditions. An example of a poor use of symbol—a computer reference book with symbols for "hot tips" and "fun facts," which were often indistinguishable. A better use of symbol in a computer reference might be to set off items "for experts only," or to distinguish descriptions of functions from examples of their uses. Often, computer and software references mix tutorials with function descriptions, causing confusion or frustration. Clearly labeling the function descriptions and distinguishing how the function is actually applied in the real world would be most helpful; a symbol to mark each description would speed the user's navigation.

Keep the symbols you do use simple, and don't use so many of them that your reader can't recall all the meanings. They should be recognizable with no effort at all. There are some bad examples of elaborate sets of icons I've seen in some books that require as much effort to decode as just reading the entire text block they serve to label! The question to ask is, "Does it add to clarity or enhance navigation, or is it merely decoration?" Purely decorative elements added to the same document with symbols that are intended to have meaning will confuse. You've probably received a flyer that makes extensive use of a variety of symbols, few of which have any role, much less any explanatory power. Sharpen your eye by taking a harder look next time you receive one of these examples; decide what you would change to make it clearer.

A word of caution: A consideration when using symbols is their interpretation across cultures. Many of us are writing for a global audience, and we have to be careful to avoid symbols that could be considered offensive or simply unintelligible. Make sure the symbols and icons you use are appropriate for the culture of your target audience.

use a metaphor

Sometimes the linear, logical approach is too dry. To get your audience's attention, suggest the idea or concept in an analogous situation. It was popular to create a Web site with "rooms" for various functions, such as a chat room or a library. You enter a chat room on the site to join others in conversation.

Online retailers have "departments" to visit. Sports or games can be used as metaphors. You've heard of people who are going on a "fishing expedition" when they are actually seeking the unknown. Think of football or baseball plays and how they can be related to life situations. Sometimes we strike out, sometimes we score a touch-

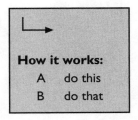

The bent arrow symbol might be used to connote an action.

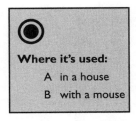

The bull's-eye might tell the reader about an application of the idea discussed.

Renovation project today

down. (OK, maybe you shouldn't mix them in one sentence.) Think of dividing a subject into parts of a puzzle, completely assembled at the end of the report or presentation. Liken your project to tending a garden, or fixing a meal. When appropriate imagery is added, a metaphor can really work to create a concept and solidify understanding.

create a matrix

A table or matrix can tell a reader a great deal in one glance. Take a situation where you want to show which of the solutions you are recommending will be the fastest and least expensive with greater long-term effects. How about a quick reference in the form of a table?

	Little long-term effect	Significant long-term effect
Fast/ Low cost	Plan A	Plan X
Slow/ High cost	Plan B	Plan Z

include an explanatory graphic or picture

Again, this is a danger zone for most of us. Graphics and pictures add beauty and color, but if they don't improve the explanatory power of your argument or description, or at least focus the viewer's eye somehow, you risk adding confusion, rather than clarity. Refer to the section on "when to use a graphic."

highlight important aspects

A simple way to make it easy on the reader—this section uses bold type for the main concept of each paragraph. The reader can scan the page and decide what to read and what to ignore.

summarize with bullets or a list

Use of numbered and bulleted lists requires forethought. Use numbered lists if the items are listed in order of importance or chronologically. You can use bullets more generically, when the items in the list have equal importance. Bullets and lists are useful for summarizing but not often for multipage laundry lists. If your list has more than fifteen or twenty bullets, you might have a few categories or groupings hidden in there!

Bullets are overused and poorly used. There should be some consistency of content and syntax among the bullets or list items. If the bullets or list items serve as options to finish a sentence, be sure to use parallel construction. All of the bullets or list elements should either be short phrases or full sentences; don't mix the two in one list. In any set of bullets or in any list, all of the items should have a common topic or relationship; don't let the content run from A to Z.

If your document will contain several sentence-length bulleted lists, don't make your reader review them all to find the one of interest to her. Highlight a key word or use a key word as the first entry on that line, followed by the complete sentence. Providing contrast is a great navigational aid for your audience. Some examples:

— This is a bullet about something, but it's hard to tell what. Good luck.

— This is a related bullet, maybe, but you'll have to read the whole thing to find out. See what I mean?

— **Dog grooming** is the subject of this bullet.

— **Dog grooming**. That's the subject of this bullet.

> Get out something you've written recently and scour it (or have an editor go over it) for any of the problems mentioned in this section. Can you detect writing habits you'd prefer to break? Use your highlighter and mark the passages in this section you need to review again the next time you start a writing project.

Basic Design

Complexity without order produces confusion; order without complexity produces boredom.

Rudolf Arnheim

design and visual logic

Graphic design creates visual logic, an organization of information with the goal of communication. When we design, we usually have more than one purpose—we want to please the eye, create interest or surprise or value. If your document has the right visual impact, it will compel the reader to continue reading. Some documents need to be text-heavy (or "gray"), and such documents must have the most careful page layout and typography. If you can offer the contrast and visual relief of properly placed graphic elements that create a visual path, your reader will have all the more motivation to continue. Err on the side of meaningless graphics, and you risk reducing the content, or information, to a subeffective, possibly counterproductive, level. To appear a credible source, your document needs a balance of useful graphics and text to keep your reader's interest; it must be attractive with contrast, white space, and clear headings. Your reader needs to perceive a logical organization that leads her through. If there is anything that can be excessive in design, it is simplicity.

composition

Composition is the arrangement of objects within a space according to some order. Composition organizes the elements, such as shape, line, tone, or color of a graphic work. Composition employs such principles as proportion, balance, and alignment to direct the observer's eye and to communicate the message. In composing your work, you determine the amount of order or disorder you will allow. The artist Roy Behrens likens extreme similarity in artwork to monotony and extreme difference to chaos. He says the artist must avoid the hum-drum just as much as the hodge-podge. The same considerations for effective composition apply whether you are creating an ad or any other printed document. Some review of basic design elements and principles will help you see your own creations more clearly.

elements of design

You make many decisions in design. The primary decision about any element of your overall design is the purpose. Just because you can add decoration does not mean it is worthwhile to do so. Every part must relate to the whole. If the elements combined fit the purpose of your creation and infuse it with meaning or value, you've done well.

line

Line can convey mood, emotion, or ideas. Lines can separate elements, suggest emotion or action, and create rhythm.

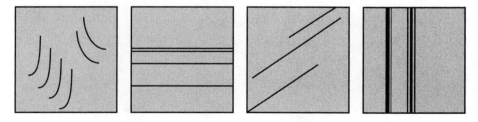

Curved lines connote gracefulness, freedom, flexibility, and rhythm. Think of all the advertisements in which you see curved lines used.

They are associating their products with freedom and flexibility for a good reason.

Horizontal lines provide harmony, stability, calm, relaxation, or a foundation. Look at advertisements and promotional materials from brokerage houses, accounting firms, and other organizations that wish to reassure you that they can be relied upon to be secure.

Diagonal lines can create tension, or evoke action, restlessness, and excitement. Diagonal lines are in suspension between a potential vertical or horizontal position.

Vertical lines achieve balance, dignity, spiritual uplift and can connote gravity or pull. Look at the sailboat regatta poster on page 214.

Look at the Web site of a major corporation, such as Lotus (www.lotus.com) or Nike (www.nike.com) and analyze the use of line.

The symbol for Nike shoes is called the *swoosh*. Why does it work or not work for you?

Find an example of the use of vertical lines and analyze why it was chosen.

positive and negative space

Positive and negative spaces have an important relationship in your creation. The area enclosed by the border of your frame is generally considered negative space. The dominant, more active forms in a composition constitute the positive space. You probably have heard of *figure* and *ground,* in which the part of a work of art we focus on is called *figure* and the surrounding area or area behind the figure is called the *ground.*

Take a new look at some of the art done by the old masters. If you do not have books with examples of work of the masters, examine paintings or artwork in your home or places you visit regularly. Study the positive and negative space in each picture.

size

Size is often used to show the importance of an object. Size is relative. We tend to compare the scale of items in a composition: larger-sized objects seem more important. Look at this classic example of the way we perceive size.

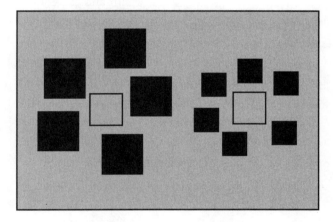

Does the open square in the center appear to be smaller next to the larger black squares?

shape

Shapes can be geometric, such as circles, triangles, or squares, or they can be free form, natural, or abstract. We usually think of a shape as a two dimensional entity.

space

Our eyes scan a work through its space. If the space is cramped or closed as opposed to open or wide, we experience it differently. Space can be flat or deep. For example, when shapes are placed parallel to the frame or border, a shallower sense of space results. A higher horizon or the overlapping of objects tends to create a sense of depth.

white space

White space, or negative space, refers to the portion of a page that is not devoted to illustration or text. It is the container for your content. Think of a rest in a piece of music, or the interval between the beams of a wall; they provide a critical function. White space is highly important to the design of the page; it gives the viewer's eye a rest. It can provide an elegant stage for the remaining elements. At times, some white space must be sacrificed for detailed information, and it is a much harder task to make anything stand out. A more detailed message requires more careful layout.

texture

Texture is the quality of the surface of an object, and the concept suggests tactile sensation. A lack of texture will usually ensure a dull result. Too much texture will overstimulate the eye. Texture provides contrast, as exemplified in collages that often employ significant amounts of texture.

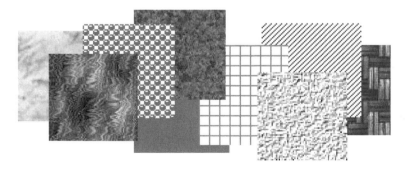

Texture offers variety

principles of design

Every design authority will supply you with a different top ten list of principles. Just relax and focus on the components that are most meaningful to you now. Reread this section later, and again still later. These principles will guide you to successful design decisions, achieving order in your composition. Of course your overall purpose, the nature of your content, and the expectations of your audience set the context of these decisions.

alignment

An arrangement of objects, when aligned, has some order. If the viewer's eye can follow a stated or unstated line, there is less confusion. This is an important concept for organizing your page. Good examples are provided in this book on pages 73 and 128.

balance

Balance is achieved when elements appear "at rest." Balance is generally considered "formal" when elements are placed in a symmetrical arrangement with an equal distribution of weight, and informal when placed in an asymmetrical arrangement. Symmetry connotes dignity and stateliness, stability, or even rigidity. Asymmetry often suggests

---

variety, movement or surprise, but many asymmetrical designs can suggest a great equilibrium. Balance can be achieved in a number of ways: a large form can balance a small one, or a splash of intense color can balance a larger expanse of dull color.

coherence

Coherence is achieved if the overall effect is a harmonious, comprehensible whole. For example: Do the colors work with the theme? With each other? Does the content hang together appropriately? As an example, I think of a hastily pulled-together report that includes some "extra" research that is tenuously tied to the main theme.

contrast

The variation from light to dark, large to small, fortissimo to pianissimo, orderly to chaotic, can create interest. A low level of contrast will connote quiet or calm. High contrast connotes excitement or drama. With respect to light/dark: you've heard the term "chiaroscuro" used when referring to films? They are highly contrasty, dramatic looking productions. Contrast is very important if you want certain things to stand out or to be easy to find. Just adding some extra white space can reduce the overall gray look of a document, for example.

**Less contrast—
nothing stands out**

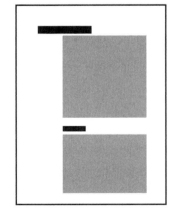

**More contrast with
bold titles and white space**

dominance

Dominance of one element draws attention to the most important area. A focal point or center of interest, needed to give the eye a place to focus, can be achieved through the use of color, position, size, shape, or a combination.

emphasis

Without emphasis, nothing stands out, and boredom can be the result. But a lack of emphasis, for example in a photograph of a lake on a foggy day, can establish an important mood or effect. Decide what you want to stress, and place the emphasis there.

flow

Flow refers to the way the arrangement leads the eye through from element to element. Using "leading lines" helps to direct your reader's eye to the place you'd like it to go. Steer the reader to each place in your creation by creating a visual path. Look at the two report covers on page 128. The Western world starts reading at the top left corner of the page and scans down and to the right. Take advantage of that natural tendency and play with it. You could use sharp, jagged lines, shapes, and space to create a jarring effect. Or, you could depict smoother transitions and softer shapes for a calmer flow.

proportion

Proportion refers to the relationships of parts of a whole, such as the overall width-height ratio or the sizes of elements within the layout. The important stuff is generally shown larger than the trivial stuff.

proximity

Proximity refers to placement of elements. If they appear together, they might be related to one another. Spatial separation can convey conceptual separation. Proximity creates clarity by grouping elements together to connote relationship to one another. Look at the subheading example on page 55. The example at right shows two lists: one is clearer than the other because elements are grouped.

FAMILY DOGS

Anna Riley

Born 11/11/97

Springer Spaniel

Amanda Panda

Born 6/20/76

Springer Spaniel

Sarah Bear

Born 4/23/74

Springer Spaniel

Rupert Birkin

Born 4/12/73

Miniature Dachshund

Bonnie Sue

Born 2/27/61

Dachshund mix

FAMILY DOGS

Anna Riley

Born 11/11/97

Springer Spaniel

Amanda Panda

Born 6/20/76

Springer Spaniel

Sarah Bear

Born 4/23/74

Springer Spaniel

Rupert Birkin

Born 4/12/73

Miniature Dachshund

Bonnie Sue

Born 2/27/61

Dachshund mix

It's difficult to determine what is listed in the example on the left while the one on the right places the supporting information for each dog right underneath the name, with space between dogs' names.

repetition

Consistency in the form of repetition is an aid to the navigation of a document, Web site, or media show. Page numbers appear in the same place on each page. Think of a Web site you visited that was inconsistent from page to page; did you wonder where you were? Setting up a style guide automates repetition. Your reader needs to know the relative importance of different pieces of information, so you signal that importance by displaying some items in larger type and bold headings with other items in smaller, normal type. Look at the partial outline view of this book on page 192. The repetition of each heading style describes the relationships between the parts of the content.

rhythm

Rhythm refers to combined repetition and variation of components in a composition. If regular, repetition can produce a calm and relaxing effect; if irregular and varied, tension and excitement can result. According to the dictionary, rhythm connotes movement characterized by the regular recurrence of strong and weak elements.

unity

Unity refers to how well the layout hangs together. What would you think if your grocery store stocked dog food, candy, and beer on the same aisle? Would you know where to go? Fortunately, the store is organized more coherently, but even if these items were found on the same aisle, signage and different shelving styles could signal their availability. Unity establishes a relationship between parts, even if the parts are quite different from one another. Repetition of headlines throughout this book establishes a unifying visual guide, uniting a variety of content types.

Get some black or very dark paper and cut out shapes—three circles, three squares, and three triangles (or choose your own shapes)—along with a long strip for a horizon line. Place each group of shapes on different white papers until you feel they are placed in pleasing relationships to one another. Move a horizon line up and down to change the feeling of depth on some of the compositions. Paste them down and compare. Place words on the back of each page describing the feeling each evokes. Did each achieve a balance, or a tension, you liked?

Page Design

We must not forget that the designer is a problem-solving person.
The problems he is to face are always given. This means he cannot
alter any of the problems but must find appropriate solutions.

Wucius Wong

elements of page design

Page design layouts are most often depicted as gray blocks (the text) against a white background (the page). For a text-heavy document, a good layout is critical to the reader's comfort and ability to navigate. You create patterns that will become familiar to the reader with the organization of elements on the page. The first thing your reader sees is not the title or other details of the page, but the overall pattern and contrast of the page, then she can begin to focus on details. Repetition is a key to navigation. If your text is organized into regular, repeating patterns, you will make it easy for the reader to learn the patterns and rhythms in your document, to predict where information is likely to be located. Clarity is enhanced also by restraint. Give your reader only what is necessary to understand the message; more gee-gaws will probably not aid understanding.

headings

Settle on as few heading styles and subtitles as are necessary to organize your content, then use your chosen styles consistently. The fact that MS Word provides multiple levels of headings doesn't mean that you should ever use them all in a single page; most likely you can avoid using more than three. Keep it simple and your document will be much easier for your reader to understand; add too many headings, indentation levels or other elements and you will scare readers off. It will attract positive attention if it looks simple.

Headings should be consistent, form a logical hierarchy, and have more space around them than normal body text. Chapter headings can be sunk far into the page in order to stand out. As with an outline, each first-level heading should have within it at least two second-level headings.

If your document must have a numbering system that adheres to military specifications, keep the numbers lighter and smaller so that the text will stand out. People looking for the numbers will find them.

1.2.1	**Heading text**
	This is the body copy.
1.2.2	**Heading text**
	This is the body copy.

subheadings

Subheadings should provide a break in the text. Adding more space above than below a subheading unites it with the copy below. In general, about twice as much space should appear above as appears below. In this book the subheadings (like the one above, "subheadings") have been defined with 14 points of space above them and with 6 points of space under them to make them look as if they belong to the paragraph that follows. These two examples tell it better:

The subheading is clearly associated with the paragraph below in the example on the right.

That's the end of the section on working dogs.

Sporting dogs

About those sporting dogs—sporting dogs are energetic and fun-

That's the end of the section on working dogs.

Sporting dogs

About those sporting dogs—sporting dogs are energetic and fun-loving. They need a

grid

A grid functions as a spatial organization system that you can use to establish a standard layout. Magazines, newspapers, phone books—printed publications in general—commonly use a grid to permit faster layouts. In the same way a master slide or template helps to organize layouts in electronic media, a grid helps the designer and the printer of paper media to produce a better product. There are no routine decisions to make about where a column will begin and end or where illustrations are to be placed. The grid divides up the space clearly and provides a procedural guide. In actuality, each page you see in the samples shown would have a graph paper look, with each small square filled in to represent the gray, or text, areas.

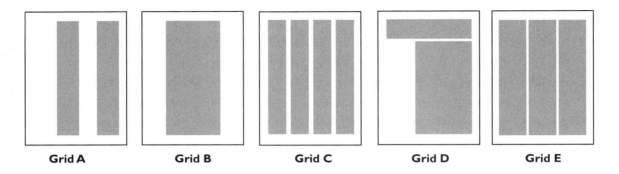

Grid A **Grid B** **Grid C** **Grid D** **Grid E**

Grid C modified

The grid is the basis for decisions, like a visual procedure. For those of us who do page layouts infrequently, the grid is a great relief from gnashing of teeth or tearing of hair (a little dramatic, maybe, but doing a layout without a grid can be trying). An illustration and some text might be two columns wide yet still work well with a multi-column format. Page through a few books and sketch out what you think the grid looks like for each. Look at an encyclopedia, a cookbook, and other books full of illustrations and then look at some periodical publications like newsletters or magazines. The grid provides the structure for the layout, and items that cross columns (like headlines, photos, illustrations, or captions) add liveliness and visual variety. The modified version of Grid C is an example. The portrait layout grids shown here could be translated to a landscape layout.

After working with a particular layout for a time, you may feel confident enough to abandon the grid. Usually those of us who don't practice design daily won't even think of doing something so rash, particularly when creating something with multiple pages or components. You can get away without using the grid for an advertisement, for example, but not in a newsletter. Your audience needs to be able to predict where to find things. Think of magazines or newspapers you can identify without ever referring to the title; you are respond-

INFORMATION DESIGN DESK REFERENCE

ing, in part, to the layout (as well as typography, color, paper, and so on.) because it is predictable.

Match the format to the content. The kind of grid you select will depend upon the information you need to present. The grids shown here depict text as gray matter to give you a better look at the spatial relationships the grid produces. If you are setting up an index for a manual, the format might be three columns, as in the example E on the far right. One of the most common formats for manuscripts is D, with all right-hand pages. (In the case of a book with both right- and left-hand pages, the left-hand page is a mirror image of the right-hand page.) Graphic elements can be placed in the margin for visual variety, or within the text area. Think about how different it would be to read this book if it used the index grid, E, for example! Or, think of how you'd find information in an index if the text ran together in paragraphs, like a book.

Say, for example, you want to create a layout for a newsletter on standard 8.5-x-11 paper, and you think you'd like to use the three-column format shown in grid E. Your word processing application allows accurate measurements of the printed page. You might set up one-inch borders with a quarter inch between columns. The resulting columns will be two inches wide. As you read on, you will be able to determine whether or not two-inch columns will work for your newsletter.

So, the grid you choose needs to be compatible with the information you are presenting. A newsletter with a number of short articles of text, with occasional accompanying illustrations, is well suited to a multicolumn format. But, if you are writing a technical description, with many formulas and examples, a three-column format might be too busy. Formats of grids A or B would work well for such a document, since examples and formulas would stand out well on the page and permit the reader to reference the information more easily.

Keep it interesting. Grids can be implicit or explicit, but you wouldn't want a border around every component of every grid. However, sometimes an occasional line of color around text looks great and adds some emphasis and contrast. Experiment, particularly if your project is an informal one, such as a brochure or poster. Sometimes, to keep it interesting, you will want to avoid sticking to the same, monotonous sequence of content. Add variety with a few horizontal breaks along with vertical columns to keep people from looking elsewhere. Try an uneven bottom margin; solve your copy-fitting dilemma and add visual interest in one operation!

Look at a magazine you like. What grid or grids are in use? Does the use of a different grid signal a different kind of content?

Create at least two grids for a project you are planning, either by sketching or by using your computer. Create the columns in each grid either in nonsense text or in gray bars. Add some headlines, subheads and graphic elements. Arrange them, rearrange them, and when you are done, compare the results.

margins

They are not a waste of space! They give final proportion to your printed product and add some needed air around the text. Some designers choose to allow graphics to "bleed" to the edge or near it, and this can be effective when used well, but for those of us who are occasional practitioners, a margin is important because it gives the reader a place for her thumbs to rest. Determining margin space in book design is a well-defined procedure, requiring mathematical calculations. If you are interested in being precise, consult Robert Bringhurst's excellent book, *The Elements of Typographic Style.*

Margins bring a balance to the page and should have a consistent relationship with the overall outline of the page, which is not to say that the text block must be placed squarely in the middle of the page! A combination of balance and contrast is key—look again at the sample grids. When the document is a book, more opportunities arise for variety among pages. The challenge with a larger project or a simpler document with all right-hand pages is to achieve a strong design that a reader can easily navigate.

runarounds

It is fairly easy to set up a runaround with most word processing software, and it does add eye relief. Make sure that you leave suffi-

cient space for text in the smaller area to prevent a loss of readability. Also, you will need to adjust text to make sure

Runaround this!

headings do not fall into place smack dab in the center of the runaround, where they will spoil the look of your document.

justification

Most documents in English are set flush left to give the eye a predict-able place to land for the beginning of each line of text. But you will need to decide whether your document should have justified or ragged right edges. The right edge in this book is ragged. I always choose rag right because I think it is easier to read, particularly if columns of writing are narrow, because the space between words is uniform. With justified type the word and letter spacing can become a bit irregular and reduce legibility, since all lines have to fill the full space of the column. Ever have a hard time reading a magazine article with narrow columns? Did it have large spaces between words to keep the right edge justified? Well, rag right can look messy, too, especially if your preference is not to hyphenate words. But most word processing programs seem to justify text pretty nicely. Notice this paragraph is right justified? Did it make any difference to you? For some of us, justified type has become more comfortable because we see it so often.

The rule generally is to set your document to ragged style if you have short lines, less than thirty-six characters. By doing so, you will avoid gulleys of white space that detract from the look of your copy. For longer lines of text, the decision is about the look of the document. Ragged-right has become popular and thus more modern looking, while justified copy tends to have a more traditional feel. There are exceptions. Experiment. A precise look with justified type could complement the most avant-garde of designs.

page numbers

Page numbers are navigational aids, and their placement can make or break their usefulness. They are easiest to find when near the top or bottom outside corner, near the text block, the same size as the text.

manipulating text blocks

line length

Long lines of text can't be read easily. Magazine and newspaper columns are narrow because the eye's span of movement is narrow. Wider lines of text require readers to read more slowly, and perhaps with more concentration. You've probably encountered lines of text so long that you couldn't find the correct next line to continue on. You were frustrated and probably quit reading. White offers some rules of thumb that have evolved over years of deciding on line length:

— 60–70 characters per line maximum

— 30 characters per line minimum

— 10 average length words (50 characters) of serif type or 8–9 words of sans serif type

If you must use a long line length, you can solve the problem by setting smaller type with larger spaces, called leading, between lines. Larger type also makes long lines easier to read.

line spacing

The typeface you use will dictate line spacing. Also called leading, line spacing is the white space between lines of text, once formed by plugs of lead in letterpress printing. Line spacing should widen as the width of the typed material increases. Normal line spacing is usually at least two points more than the body-copy size. The text you are reading now is 11-point Garamond with 14 points of leading. If your body copy is 10-point type, the spacing between lines should be 12 or 13 points with about a space and a half between paragraphs.

Strive to make the patterns formed by the text pleasing to the eye. Each line of text needs to be defined from neighboring lines, but not so much that the reader must work hard to find the next line. Proportions of the typeface you select will help you choose the appropriate point size for your product; different typefaces require significantly different amounts of space, vertical and horizontal.

— Type with long **ascenders** and **descenders**, the extensions that go up or down from the body of the letter, need much more leading than a more standard-looking typeface. In the lists of letters below, think about the amount of space you prefer, in order to keep the ascenders and descenders from interfering with one another visually.

Lowercase letters with descenders: g, j, p, q, y
Lowercase letters with ascenders: b, d, f, h, k, l, t

— The height of the center part of letters must be taken into account, too. Allow more spacing between lines if the "**x-height**" is taller (the letter x has no ascender or descender, thus, "x-height"). Arial has a larger x-height and needs larger leading as a result.

kerning

There are many other measures associated with typesetting that can alter the look of the printed word. When type was set by hand, it was important to get the letter spacing right, to make sure the result was readable. It is reassuring to know that you don't need to be concerned about spacing between letters in a word, called kerning, because it can be done for you by your computer's word processing software, although you can override this function. Some letters are always placed closer to one another to make them look right within a word. For example, capital *Y* or *T* should overhang a nearby *o* or *a*.

sentence spacing

Another thought, about sentence spacing. I still use the old-fashioned two spaces after a sentence. However, it is thought much more modern, and it has become standard, to use one space. I like the extra space because it signals a pause, indicating that one thought is finished. We tend to pause between spoken sentences, so it seems natural to do it between written sentences. Use of two spaces between sentences is rare now, as it is considered a waste of space; perhaps that became fully entrenched in the early days of computers, when a space took up more memory than we could afford to give up. Select spacing between sentences that works for you, and be consistent. One exception: never use two spaces at the end of sentences if you right-justify text; you will see large white spots in the gray text areas that will spoil the look of your document.

headings

Editorial landmarks like titles and headers are the chief navigational aids in any print publication, rather than icons, banner graphics, bullets, horizontal rules. A consistent approach to the titles, headlines, and subheads in your documents will aid your readers far more than gimmicks. Once the reader has become accustomed to the overall style of text and layout, he will be able to find topics easily. Icons or bullets are less useful for navigation through a document because they give the reader another task to perform to read your message.

Headings and subheadings not only break up the gray landscape of text, but they provide transition between content elements. It would be difficult to think of a useful segue from "headings" to "lists" here other than a subheading!

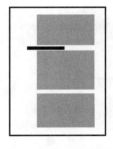

two heading styles

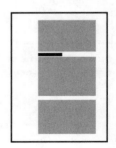

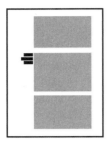

subheading without heading

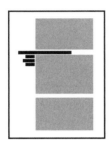

subheading with heading

bullets for items of equal importance

Use downstyle (set like a sentence with capitalization only for the first word) to aid legibility for headers. Then, set headings apart from normal text by increasing the type size, or by using boldface, or by using a different typeface. Placement is a matter of opinion, since it depends upon the look of the body text. I like hanging-indent headings because they stand out in the large white margin, helping the reader to refer to a topic of interest. Another style that would work here is the side head, where the header text is set next to the body text, as shown in the example. Note the flush-right set. I have to admit, I like the look of the side head better, but it is a more work to manipulate in a word processing program.

Headings can be centered, set in a box, placed at the left side of the body text, or even set as a runaround. All can work very well, as long as the treatment is clear. Headings are a key clue to navigating your document. Keep the headings and the hierarchy of headings you use consistent. Create a dummy document with the headings and body text, and play with it to see what you like best.

lists

Lists provide a navigational aid to the reader. They're easy to find on the page because they're highlighted, indented or "outdented," and the lines are usually short. Lists allow readers scanning the document to gather clues to content. If the lead-in describes the topic clearly, the list is understood to be an explanation of the topic. (Refer to Clarifying Information for a treatment of bullet and list content.)

There are several conventions for listed items beyond numerals and bullets. You can use dashes, symbols, outline format, or simple indentation. Often, a list can stand on its own without the addition of any mark beside the words. For example, a sequential list can simply start with the words *First, Second,* and so on.

How do you make lists look right on the page? The number or bullet should stand out, and all of the text on the left should line up together, as in the example shown. If the list has long phrases or sentences, a capital letter should lead off. A list item should have a period at the end if it is a full sentence. Lists with multiple lines per item tend to look better right justified, if the rest of your document is justified. Lists with only a few words per item are naturally best set rag-right, even if the rest of the document is right justified.

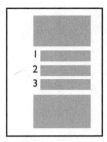

numbers for items
- in chronological order
- in order of importance

paragraphs

Paragraphs contain a set of related items of information. Sometimes long text passages are broken up rather arbitrarily into paragraphs. Whatever the use, paragraphs need some kind of landmark to signal a pause. Indents are considered a requirement by many editors. If you use an indent, make it a modest one. Widely **indented first lines** are hard to locate and, when they follow a short last line, they can spoil the look of the page. Although I don't like them, out-dented paragraphs can work, too. This document uses a full line-space to signal a new paragraph. Book editors and those conserving paper cannot always be so generous with space. Plus, you may agree with Robert Bringhurst's assertion that **block style** is good for memos and short documents but is "soulless" and uninviting in longer documents. Obviously, I disagree (although I do feel Bringhurst is right on almost everything). Have a look at some printed publications and decide what you like best, if you're not already firmly wedded to a paragraph style.

pagination

Pagination is important to the overall look. Avoid widow lines—those are the last lines of paragraphs on the top of a following page. Use at least two lines of a previous paragraph at the top of a page. Bringhurst recommends balancing pages by moving entire lines, not by hiding additional spaces between lines or words. If a few pages run a line short, that's fine.

copyfitting

Copyfitting was once a laborious endeavor, involving counting all the characters inside and outside the bounds of your margins and completing a few arithmetic manipulations to determine the total number of characters. Now, your word processing program will count words, letters, spaces, and lines for you. If you know the letter spaces and lines available, you can rewrite or edit your copy to fit. It's still time-consuming, and it's still a challenge, but we have it much easier now! Also, word processing applications allow us to change the size of typeface to make it fit the available space. Remember, the numbers of different type sizes should be minimal. And if you are setting the majority of your brochure in 8-point type, you need a larger brochure or less copy.

If your **document will be translated** into other languages, be sure to allow extra space. I've read estimates of up to 40 percent extra space for other languages. English is more compact than many other languages.

shorter documents

Shorter documents must be concise and structured for fast scanning. The "inverted pyramid" style used in journalism works well. Get the important facts up near the top of the first paragraph where readers can find them quickly. Use lists, tables, or charts for supporting detail.

longer documents

Longer documents require the strictest adherence to an overall style or established set of type style settings used consistently throughout. Consistency gives polish and encourages the reader to continue by establishing an expectation of the structure of a text. If this expectation is not met due to inconsistent formatting, readers will not have a comfortable experience and may give up.

style-setting

I was once responsible for coordinating input to create a design standards document for a building. No one had to guess about office sizes, counter heights, lighting fixtures, finishes, and so on. Everything was defined. There are many benefits to establishing a style before creating a document, presentation, or Web site, too. Chief among them is enhancing the user's ease of navigation by establishing a visual hierarchy. Word-processing packages have default styles that you can modify, or you can start over with your own creation. The beauty of automated style setting is its uniformity—you can do less thinking about structure and more thinking about content.

Styles also permit fast outline views of your creation, invaluable when creating a longer document. You can generate an accurate, dynamic table of contents, too, when you use a style. Once you have decided how you want your printed page or presentation to look, you can use the style editor to create just what you want. Play with the style function in your word-processing application to decide on settings such as typeface, inter-paragraph spacing, the size of subheads, and so on. Create a style sheet you like to help you maintain these settings throughout your document. This is especially critical for large documents with numerous pages. Create a short document like the one

below and use it to create exactly the look you want. Change the
style, and you will see an entirely different look.

Title-Heading 1

Heading 2
Normal normal normal normal normal normal normal
normal normal

Sub heading 3
Normal normal normal normal normal normal normal
normal normal normal normal normal normal normal

○ Bullet
○ Bullet
○ Bullet

No style applied

Title-Heading 1
Heading 2
> Normal normal normal normal
> normal normal normal

Sub heading 3
> Normal normal normal normal
> normal normal normal normal
> normal normal normal

■ Bullet
■ Bullet
■ Bullet

With a style applied

INFORMATION DESIGN DESK REFERENCE

emphasis with text

A simple way to add navigational cues is to emphasize text in a consistent manner. When you emphasize text, you give clues to the meaning and add landmarks for the reader. Each technique has pros and cons:

CAPITALS, as you will see in the chapter on Type and Legibility, can become obstacles for the reader, since we look for the silhouette of a word as we read. Use them sparingly to provide emphasis in short bursts. You have to slow down and concentrate to read them. That's why newspapers have headlines in all caps.

Boldface gives strong emphasis. Boldface is best used sparingly within body text (to get attention) or it can be used for titles and headings.

Italics can be useful for titles, quotations, foreign words, or breakouts that need to be differentiated from body text. Italics are often overused; we think that italics add emphasis, when they actually reduce legibility. They can add an attractive element to your document, so save them for additional or less important information that you do not want to distract from your main point.

Underlined words do not have as strong an appearance as boldface, and should be used sparingly. They don't offer the contrast you may wish for. Some word-processing programs place extra space between lines where underlining occurs. And underlines always intersect the letters' descending strokes, impeding readability.

Increase the size of the type. Gets your attention, doesn't it? Again, don't overdo this one! Use only a few sizes of type in one document. Changing the size of the type will change the line spacing.

Use a different typeface sparingly. Too many elements and typefaces will make your document look amateurish. The pros can really go wild combining oddly shaped, asymmetrical type with other sorts of type. It is difficult for most of us to combine or use highly irregular type successfully.

Color provides emphasis, but it should provide some clue to meaning, too. If it is used only for decoration, try the document without it first and then add it sparingly. If you need color to attract attention, think about exactly the attention you want to attract. For those of us not expert in the use of color, it is best to err on the conservative side. Note that the word color here is gray, since this section is in black and white. If you photocopy a document, the words you set in color could end up looking less important!

Think of letters as forms or shapes with positive and negative space. Just for fun, illustrate one of the words in this list by hand lettering, adding any other touches you'd like: speed, jazz, hot, nervous, broken, chaotic, crescendo, snake, skip, forté.

Try varying letter positions, size, alignment, and contrast between characters and see if you can find the typeface with the right "voice" to characterize the word.

direct the reader's eye

In designing information, your objective is to control the viewer's eye in order to lead her clearly to your message. In the West, readers of English read from left to right and from the top of the page to the bottom. The professor of an advertising class I took said that the typical page scanning pattern actually forms a Z. But this habit of left to right eye movement dominates most design decisions and is the basis for most conventional graphic design of print publications. In page layout the top of the page is the most dominant location. Your **focal point** should dominate the layout in the area where reader's eyes naturally begin. If you have more than one dominant element or focal point, your reader has to guess where to start, and you can lose him.

The elements in your design should flow, making the reader's eye go from element to element in a course that you direct. If you organize and sequence the information logically, and you provide meaning, the document will function appropriately.

Color can aid navigation, but if you are new to graphic design and color selection, choose subtle pastel shades of colors typically found in nature, particularly for minor elements. Use caution with bold primary colors, even when you want to achieve maximum emphasis. Type must always contrast sharply with a background color. If you have a highly complex graphic scheme in mind, hire a professional graphic designer to execute it. If you are not a designer and must do it yourself, keep everything conservative and simple.

Remember that people often skim or skip through a document to find something worth reading, and this practice is far more prevalent on the Web. The markers they find should have explanatory power, that is, they should be integral to the content. Decorative graphics, such as graphic bullets, icons, and other visual markers have their occasional uses, but they can create confusion rather than enhancement. Overuse of graphics for emphasis can become garish and end up defeating the purpose. Use graphic elements to pull the eye toward the most important information, or toward the elements that follow in a sequence. A line used this way, called a leading line in art or photography, guides viewers in the direction you set.

Remember the description of establishing a layout grid and a style for handling your text and graphics? Stick with it to build a consistent rhythm or pattern and unity within the document. Repetition gives your site a consistent graphic identity that reinforces a distinct sense of "place," making your document more memorable. A consistent approach to layout, and a clear visual hierarchy, allows readers to quickly adapt to your design and to confidently predict the location of information.

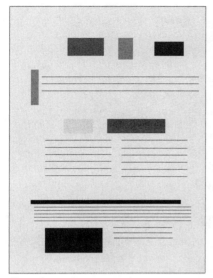

Poor layout—
everything is floating freely,
without alignment.

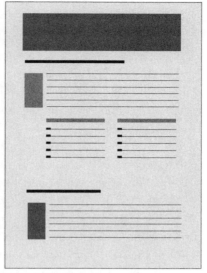

Better layout—
alignment helps the reader locate
information, and better use of white
space provides more contrast.

There are some easy ways to make your document or presentation stand out. It doesn't take much to add some shading or rule lines, or (oh boy, I'm afraid to suggest…) **boxes**. About the boxes. They are ubiquitous and not often very attractive. Here are some tips.

Use shading to add some depth. Be careful with gradient effects if you plan to photocopy the work or post it on the Web, because you will probably be disappointed. But a shaded background can make text boxes pop out and make it easier to follow the data in a table. Note the drop-shadow behind the box? Use these with restraint. The idea is to depict a light source in a corner in the example.

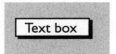

Shading can make
elements stand out

If another element is added to the page with a drop shadow with the "light source" coming from another direction, the overall effect is sloppy.

See, I'm not against boxes. Just abuse of boxes. Use them for sidebars and when the situation really merits a box! If you put everything in a box, everything will look as random as it would without any boxes.

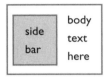

Horizontal rule lines can signal a break in the content. Horizontal lines follow the direction of text and offer welcome relief to the eye. Be careful of too many verticals, or your document will look like a tic-tac-toe game. Keep the lines plain and vary the weight if you use them for more than one purpose. Don't assume that rule lines are like underlines. Try using them above the text you wish to set off and farther away from the text.

Lines offer some relief for the eye

developing your layout

Here are the bare bones steps to getting your layout done.

1   **Define the purpose:**
    What is the intended outcome?

2   **Analyze the target audience:**
    How will this interest them? (Go back to the checklist.)

3   **Describe the main and supporting points:**
    What is the main message you want to convey? Write it in one short
    sentence. Write down the supporting messages.

4   **List where it will be seen/distributed:**
    The poster is seen by random passers-by, while a brochure might be
    targeted toward a specific trade show audience. Even with the same
    topic, content, and look, a brochure versus a poster would be quite
    different.

5   **Establish the concept:**
    What creative visual idea exemplifies your message? Goof around!
    Really! Have some fun and look at as many different pictures, illus-
    trations, or things as you can to get some stimulation. Then, try a
    different concept and look at visuals to support it. Which one
    works? Which one do you like better?

6 **Research content:**
Get as much exposure to the content as you can so that you can understand it fully. The more you know, the more dimensions you can bring to the final product.

7 **Write copy/content:**
Write succinctly, drawing from your main and supporting messages. Is the content complete? Edit ruthlessly.

8 **Organize information into logical groups:**
You may already have this done if you are basing your writing on the supporting messages you want to convey. If you have many supporting messages, your document had better be important enough to warrant them.

9 **Select layout elements:**
Give some thought, and emotion, to the nontext elements, such as charts, photographs, or illustrations. Think about color, placement, size, and make sure they amplify the meaning of your text. Remember that we tend to look at the brightest, highest contrast and heaviest elements first. Allow your "gut" to tell you if you are achieving the feel of the subject.

10 **Experiment with layout variations:**
By using separate components, you can rearrange them and find the layout—design—you like. Cut the text up into chunks by idea, too. Place text chunks and the associated graphics near one another. Establish a visual hierarchy. Consider where you want the viewer to look first, second, and third and create a visual path to ensure that they are looking in that sequence. And take some chances! Try something new, instead of staying locked into the old same thing. Emphasize the focal point! Make it stand out by making it a stronger, brighter color, a different value, a different texture, a different shape, a different opacity, whatever. Or make it stand out because everything revolves around it or points to it. But have only one focal point. (Focal point "overload" is a pet peeve of mine. I think of clothing design, particularly, where a large bow, a ruffle, and a wide belt all clamor for attention, and one doesn't know where to look first.)

11 **Photocopy different layouts:**
There's no better way to find a great layout if you're not using any kind of drawing software. Look at it several ways before you commit to one. Remember that we read, both print and visuals, from left to right and from the top of the page. Remember that professor's recommendation to imagine your reader scanning the page in the shape of a Z.

12 **Evaluate the selections:**
Go back to the design principles and check your work against them. For example:
Unity: Do graphics tie in with content?
Repetition: Are repeated elements used consistently to create continuity?
Emphasis: Is the focal point obvious?
Flow: Is there a clear visual path?
Then, ask a potential member of your target audience to look at it and tell you what message is conveyed and how easily it can be read.

An actual yellow pages ad (names changed to protect perpetrator) and another layout for the same information, using essentially the same typeface and main graphic element. The one on the right isn't perfect either, but it is less confusing to look at because the main message isn't buried in shouting capitals and conflicting graphics.

graphic placement

Before you begin to place graphics, you must decide where you want the visual emphasis. What is important in your message? In documents or sections of documents that feature graphics, drawing a rough layout is a good aid to visualizing the final look. Here's a rough layout for the inside of a three-fold brochure. I like to create a rough sketch in my word-processing or presentation software to make it easy to move elements around, size them, or delete them. The body text can be represented as gray boxes, headlines as thicker lines, and illustrations can be represented as boxes with an **X**.

A word of caution: it is faster for most people to draw these representations! If you aren't accustomed to using the drawing features, don't waste time getting frustrated. Sketch it and then do a near final on the computer. What you will appreciate about placing your layout in your word-processing application is the ability to view it in context with the print preview feature, which shows a thumbnail view of the pages in your document.

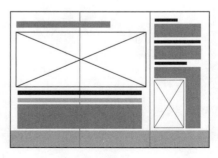

In this brochure, two of the sections will contain a shared graphic and accompanying test.

**flush
left**

**flush
right**

It is best to use flush left or flush right placement for headings and graphics. I like to think of it as having a hinge upon which things can hang and flip one way or the other; the hinge provides an anchor in space so that elements do not appear to be free floating. (Free-floating text can be done effectively, but it requires some know-how.) Centering elements within a column is less effective because white space is broken; it is better to combine white space into one larger unit. Also, the reader's rhythm of returning to the beginning of the line is broken.

A very useful guideline offered by the *Xerox Publishing Standards* is to maintain the integrity of the vertical scanning area and the right margin. Xerox defines the following **rules for placing graphics** (numbers correspond to the blocks in the following illustration):

1   Place a **small** graphic flush right with the column of text. Closeness indicates belonging together.

2   Place a graphic that is **same width as text column** flush right and left justified.

3   If the graphic is **narrower than the text column,** place it flush left within the text column.

4   Limit the **area of an illustration** to the width of the margins of the document.

5   If the graphic is **wider than the text column,** place it flush right within the text column and let it extend into the white space, which is called the scanning column.

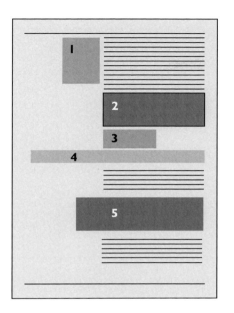

Size and shape are considered when a placing a graphic element in a layout with text.

This layout needs your help. What would you change or omit, assuming you will keep the basic information?

typeface and fonts

Few among us have the time or desire to design a new typeface. Those of us who just want to learn to use them properly, rather than create great typographic art, can do so easily enough. Our primary goal is the message, rather than the form of delivery. The best type-faces are easy to read and attractive and don't impede the reader's progress. The anatomy of type is shown here. We'll be referring to some of the terms used later on.

There are two major families of type, sans serif and serif:
Sans serif type, like Arial, has no feet.
Serif type, like Century Schoolbook, has feet.

Serif type is said to be easier on the eye. That's probably why we learned to read books set in Century Schoolbook, which works well in short passages of text, like your first primer. The serifs, which I've read originated in sloppy chisel technique on stone monuments, blend words together with their horizontal lines. In sans serif type, the letters stand as individual elements.

Look at a document that uses a sans serif style for body text. The letters in sans serif type are undifferentiated—each stroke is about the same weight, and there are no flourishes at the ends of strokes. We really do rely on these subtle differences in the weight of different letter strokes to recognize letters quickly.

combining typefaces

Using a serif typeface for body text and a sans serif for contrasting headlines, just as you see in this book, is a fairly standard treatment. There's no magic answer, and you will not be arrested for mixing type, just as it's OK to use only one. In fact, you will encounter numerous examples of mixed typefaces: Helvetica, Arial, or Gill is often combined with a variety of serif styles. It's a good idea to copy the same heading and body text onto several pages and create combinations of type to compare. Generally, if it looks right, it is.

To keep your work simple, you should use no more than two typefaces in any document (the pros get away with more); in the two examples shown, a sans serif heading is used for one while a serif type matching the body text is used in the other. Note that two different serif types or two different sans serif types are not combined; it would only look messy. And sans serif type is rarely used as body text in paper documents. If you are very particular, a good guideline to follow, when using two typefaces, is to stay within a family of type. Within a family the general size and shape of letters is fairly consistent. The Lucida family, for example, is enormous including calligraphy, script, sans serif, and serif typeface.

Note the same basic shape of the letters of the serif and sans serif varieties.

Lucida fax
Lucida sans
Lucida bright
Lucida calligraphy

I included the calligraphy style to make another point. As a general rule, don't use an ornate or script style typeface along with other type. This stuff needs to stand alone.

selecting typefaces

Each typeface has a variety of uses. Some are more limited. You would not set an entire document in script, blackletter, or novelty type because your reader would give up after a short time. Specialty and decorative typefaces can certainly set a mood, but they are often difficult to read. Examples of type more suited to long passages of text are Optima, Times Roman, Helvetica, Caslon, Minion, and Garamond (the last one is used here). There are many others. If you know of a book you thought to be set in an excellent typeface, find out the name and use it! As you gain experience with type you will settle on a type style for your documents.

In addition to type styles, there are a multitude of variations, such as boldface, light, wide, and condensed. You can choose one typeface and vary its size and weight throughout a document. If you don't dare take a chance on making a decision, go with the classics. Still need some direction with typeface? Consider the following in your selection:

— Audience

— Content

— Mood

— Graphics

— Overall amount of text

I've seen many prescriptions for typeface use, such as sans serif for technical writing, for example. I don't think there's a reason to limit yourself to a narrow range, but you do need to match the content with the type. They can all convey a style and a mood. You would not ordinarily choose an **ornate** type style for a brochure describing an exhibit of contemporary art. The subject and the type need to agree with one another; it is riskier to choose a contrast, but it's not illegal. Get another opinion. This book gives the most traditional, conservative advice because business people (a likely audience for this book) seek credibility.

For example, what kinds of type do you see when a friendly tone is projected? A nice fat rounded type. I got sick of seeing **comic sans** everywhere a few years back. It was often used inappropriately when the tone of the content was far from friendly.

Look at the type style and subjects in the poster mock-ups below. Type has a "voice." That voice should complement the other elements. The tool show poster could use a heavier, stronger looking typeface. The flower show poster might look better with a more graceful or fluid typeface, and the antique show poster could use a less modern looking typeface, although the wild typeface shown could work. Rules can be broken, of course. After you've had some experience you might find a way to create interest with an unexpected look.

Tool Show

Flower Show

ANTIQUE SHOW

Choose a typeface for one of the posters. Assess a few sample typefaces from different viewpoints. You can distinguish fine differences between typefaces by selecting one letter, an *e* or an *o* for example, and comparing one type to one another. (This is a useful technique for combining typefaces, too.) To get the big picture, simply place entire words next to the graphics and compare the effects.

Of the typefaces you have seen, which would best connote different conditions or moods, such as joy, violence, drama, romance?

Check some movie advertisements and decide whether or not the typeface fits the expected mood of the movie.

photocopies

Will you need to have photocopies of your document made? Many serif typefaces do not copy well because the thinner strokes tend to disappear in reproduction. Sans serif typefaces usually have strokes of more even thickness. While we're on the topic of copying, there is the problem of type (serif or sans) with small "counters"—that's the word for the hole inside letters like *o, a,* or *g.* Refer to the anatomy of type chart on page 83. Try to choose type with larger counters, because small holes tend to fill up with ink when a copy is made, making your document very difficult to read.

font v. typeface

When you have narrowed down the typefaces you plan to use in your various documents, you need to think about font. Sometimes the word "font" is used interchangeably with "typeface," and in reality they are different. A font is a full set (including numbers and symbols) of any one size and style of type, such as 12-point Helvetica, bold. Again, keep the number of fonts down. Use no more than three sizes of one type within a page and no more than five in a document. Too many sizes and kinds of typeface will confuse your reader.

body text size

Decide on the size of your body text. A little background on the point system is used to describe type dimensions: One point is 0.01383 inch and there are 12 points to a pica and 72 points to an inch, or 6 picas. Generally, the size of document type goes up to 14 point, and beyond 14 point, type is considered "display" type (some authorities draw the line at 12 points). The *Xerox Publishing Standards* recommends 10-point Optima type for reference material, 11-point Optima type for student materials, and 12-point Optima type for instructor materials, since instructors are often at some distance from their manuals. (They specify the style of type because it is the corporate standard and because the size of typeface can vary.)

Many books use extremely large type for the text and get away with it; you'll notice that they tend to have lots of large graphic elements, too. But the standard historically has been 10 point, and you should make a decision based upon the look of your chosen typeface and the space between lines, width of columns, size of the page, the overall amount of text in the document, and so on. For this and any of your decisions, "Keep it simple" is a useful motto. There is a formula if you want to be more scientific about type size. The rule of thumb is to make the type half the measure of the line length—so, if your line measures 20 *picas* in length (roughly three inches), make the type 10 point. But if you add some space between longer lines, you can still use 10-point type and get away with it. Lines in this book are a bit longer, so I chose 11 point, instead of the 10 point you see in this sentence.

One last word: any type used in call-outs or footers should be smaller than the body text. The smallest point size I have available is 8. However, 8 point might be too small for some typeface. Test!

type and legibility

We read by recognizing the overall shape of words, relying upon the bumpy shapes of their outlines that catch our eye. That's why the size of the body of a letter, known as the x-height, is an important consideration. Type with smaller x-heights, such as Bernhard Fashion may need to be set in a larger size to be legible. This is Bernhard Fashion set in 14 point. Notice how the x-heights in 14 point approach the size of the 11-point Garamond used in this book. Bernhard Fashion requires extra space.

In type with taller x-heights, lowercase n's and h's can look very similar, and legibility can suffer. For example, you can tell the word "hot" from "not" easily when set in Times Roman, as in the example. But isn't it a little more work to tell them apart when they're set in AvantGarde?

hot not

hot not

Capitals do get attention, but the experts recommend avoiding all uppercase, for the most part. It works for a very brief headline because the square shape forces the reader's eye to slow down. Think of a STOP sign, for example. For a body of text, however, uppercase lettering is much harder to read because the outlines of words formed with capital letters are monotonous rectangles that offer few distinctive shapes to catch the reader's eye. This, now classic, illustration clarifies the difference in "topography!"

CAPITALS ARE RECTANGULAR while lower case is bumpy.

Another word about capitals: use all caps in an email message and your recipients will think you're shouting. Capitals should be used sparingly. Even the use of initial capital letters in your subtitles can potentially disrupt the reader's ability to recognize words:

Initial Caps Distract

Legibility depends on the tops of words; uppercase or lowercase letters can have a dramatic effect on legibility. Using downstyle (just like a sentence: capitalize only the first word, and any proper nouns) for your headlines and subheads improves legibility, because, as several of the authorities I have consulted agree, we scan the tops of words as we read. Here's another classic illustration:

Legibility depends upon recognizing the tops of words

Try to read the bottom half of the same sentence:

Legibility depends upon recognizing the tops of words

Color

To paint well is simply this: to put the right color in the right place.

                                        Paul Klee

color basics

Color has great power. Color has temperature. It can evoke emotion, and it can even change appetite. It is not to be used haphazardly. But how often is color really managed well?

Artists study the nature of color in the way that musicians learn to read musical notation. Music is a useful metaphor for the use of color. Imagine a piece of music played at a fortissimo, or extra loud level, throughout. It would become rather uninteresting! But fortissimo sections interspersed through a variety of volume levels would hold a listener's interest. Color is much the same. Strong loud colors, all used together, will probably create a violent and disturbing effect. You might want to create that effect at times, or you might want to present a more harmonious use of color. How do you create excitement or harmony? We'll start with a little background on color basics.

value, depth, and temperature

The study of color is a course in itself. For example, color has value (from light to dark), depth (it can appear to recede or advance), temperature (we see reds as warm, blues as cold), and relative intensity.

Exercise in value

Value: Looking at the sample here is fine, but try the exercise yourself, if you have a simple set of watercolors (or you can use a drawing program). Divide a long rectangle into row of five one-inch squares, lightly using a pencil on watercolor paper. Choose any color (red, blue, green, yellow, orange, purple...pick your favorite) and fill in the middle square with that straight color. Fill in the next square (to the left) with the same color, but add a bit of white to it. Fill in the next square with even more white added to the original color. On the right side, add successively more black. You have demonstrated that lightening or darkening color (changing a color's value) is easy. It is done by adding white to form a **tint**, or by adding black to form a **shade**. Do you notice the effect the colors have on one another? Do you see bands within each square that make the side next to the lighter color appear darker, and the side next to the darker color appear lighter? Artists use this effect for emphasis. Why do you think contour maps of ocean depths or land elevations place dark lines between the different gradations of color?

Which circle appears closer?

Depth: You can try this exercise with watercolors and watercolor paper, or in your drawing program. Draw a simple shape, like a square or circle, in the center of a square. Duplicate this drawing and color the background a dark color on one, and make the central shape dark on the other. You should see how lighter colors seem to be closer, and for that reason somewhat larger. I just created the illustration (next to this exercise) and had to copy the darker circle and place it over the white one to PROVE to myself that I hadn't inadvertently made the white one bigger! The white one definitely appears closer.

Vivid and grayed shades of red

The **intensity** of a color is related to the light waves that comprise it. A pure color is considered intense; or you might hear the words "saturated" or "vivid," which have similar meanings. An intense color is as far from gray as possible. Think of adding gray to a vivid red; you would reduce its intensity and make it dull.

One key to using color well is learning how color is modified. We can do this by mixing hues or by using colors together. There are other ways, such as varying the texture of a surface, or changing the light in the room, but we'll just cover the first two.

the color wheel

There are a few color grouping systems; the most commonly mentioned system is the color-wheel system, which has been around since 1730. The color wheel has within it the three **primary hues** (or colors), red, yellow, and blue. It also contains the **secondary hues**, produced by mixing approximately equal parts of primary hues. For example, secondary hues include orange, which is obtained by mixing red and yellow. In addition, a primary hue can be mixed with a secondary hue to form an **intermediate,** or **tertiary, hue,** such as yellow-orange or blue-green.

color wheel

At the center of some representations of the color wheel sits a **neutral hue,** formed by equal parts of the primary hues. As a kid, I remember creating a lot of gray and brown when I tried to mix color; that's what happens when you mix two complements, such as red with green.

color schemes

One aspect of color management, using colors together, is an important basis for helping you get the color scheme you want for your output. The main schemes are described briefly here:

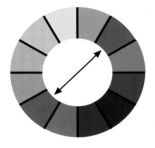 

In **complementary color schemes** colors that appear directly across from one another on the color wheel, farthest away from one another, called complements, are juxtaposed. Examples of complementary color schemes include violet and yellow, blue and orange, or red and green. Complementary colors provide excitement. They seem to vibrate (some would say quarrel) when placed in juxtaposition and stimulate the eyes significantly. In general, these color schemes look best when one color dominates and the other is an accent, taking less than one quarter of the space of the page. Or, if you don't want as strong an effect, they can be used together successfully when one or both of the colors is "de-saturated," that is, duller or less vivid. One very important issue to remember is color "blindness," which is really more correctly termed color deficiency. Difficulty with red-green distinctions is the most common, affecting about 10 percent of all males; never use red and green in situations where distinguishing between the two colors is critical.

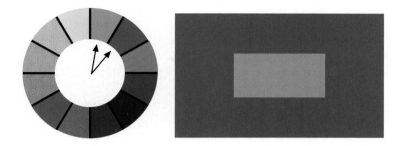

Analogous color schemes use related colors, those that are adjacent to each other on the color wheel. The effect is somewhat softer, more peaceful or harmonious; these color schemes are the safest to use when you are unsure, since they are unlikely to clash. Generally these color schemes are chosen from either the cool or the warm hues. Think of room décor: imagine a kitchen with yellow walls, yellow-green accents, and darker-green plants and pictures. Might not be your favorite, but it would hang together well. In addition, it would be a calmer kitchen than, say, a yellow kitchen with magenta accents. See what I mean? Helps to use the home as an example.

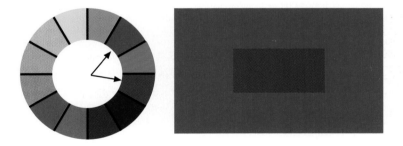

Contrasting color schemes, using colors separated by two or three other colors on the color wheel, can produce bold or vivid effects. If you established this scheme in a child's play room, you might use more equal amounts of the various colors for some punch. If you were to use this scheme in an adult activity room, you might use splashes of some colors with another dominant color.

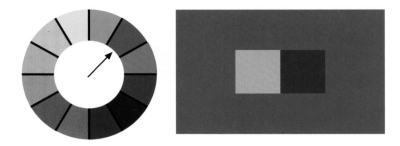

Monochromatic color schemes use the shades and tints of one color. The effect is usually subdued and can be sophisticated, elegant, calm, and soothing-or dull. Think of a room with furnishings and wall color in variations of one basic color. Probably this isn't a playroom. More likely it's an office or sitting room.

Warm v. cool color schemes. Cool color schemes can be restful and may recede to the background while warm color schemes call attention to themselves, advance to the foreground, and induce excitement. Have you ever seen a room in several cool tones or several warm tones? How did each make you feel?

No color scheme is inherently more esthetically pleasing than another. Like all the elements of a final product, color is best when used consistently. Done carefully, color can be a way to emphasize a document's organization.

Cut some shapes from a variety of colored construction papers. Then put the shapes colors together in experimental combinations against full sheets of color as background. Move them around and change the background color. Take note of how the intensity of the color appears to change, depending upon the color you use as background.

Review with others a selection of graphics or colorful images that appeal to you or to which you react negatively. Find out what others like or do not like and why. Ask them to say how a change in dominant color or shift to more muted or bright tones would alter the message of an image or graphic. Take note of how your opinions compare to those of others.

Find an art book and look at some paintings—Monet, for example. Look for the use of complementary colors to depict light on flowers, a building, a hillside. He softens them with white, but the effect is a shimmer. Or, look at the soft green trees Corot painted next to people wearing a bit of a slightly more vivid red. Think about how different their paintings would look if another color had been chosen for an element.

INFORMATION DESIGN DESK REFERENCE

popular connotations of colors

We have strong associations in our minds with colors, usually cultur-
ally bound. We are all consciously or unconsciously aware of the
meaning of color. Red and orange tones are dominant: they shout at
us, conveying urgency or danger. You might think of road signs.
But you would never think of red for a relaxing illustration of a kitty
curled up in a favorite chair. Extra bright tones connote high tech or
modernity. Blues, grays, and browns recede into a page and convey a
very safe message. Traditional businesses, like accounting firms, have
relied on these colors to let us know how stable and reliable they are,
but this practice has begun to shift as tastes shift. Pastels are associated with gentleness and femininity. A poster about a tool show
would not look credible in light pink; masculine colors, which are
similar to the old reliable colors, would be a better choice for that
poster. Interestingly, sophistication is also conveyed with blues,
grays, browns, and wine tones, with a small amount of metallic for
eye relief and subtle excitement. Earth tones are used to connote
natural foods, strength, and healthy living.

So, colors have meanings and feelings associated with them. Culture,
history, and experience define our attitudes toward color. Color can
be controversial, and meanings are inconsistent and constantly in

---

flux! The interpretations shown below are simply opinions, or connotations shaped by our culture. Use the space next to the popular interpretation to write your own thoughts about the color and what you feel is the best use of that color. There is no formula, and the best course of action, if you are unsure, is to gather several opinions.

	Color	Connotations	Your preference for best use
	Red	emotion, urgency, excitement, fear, hazards, energy, determination, passion, courage, health, danger, power, financial loss, prostitution, guilt, virility, sin, embarrassment	
	Orange	happiness, courage, success, liveliness, excitement, Halloween, autumn	
	Yellow	enthusiasm, play, optimism, cheerfulness, creativity, cowardice, treason, deceit, contagion, bad luck, caution	
	Gold	illumination, wisdom, wealth, luminosity	
	Brown	naturalness, strength, health, stability, earthiness, practicality, reliability, masculinity, bad taste, contemplation	

Gray	self-denial, neutrality, simplicity, experience, age, sickness	
Silver	positive, stability, optimism, intelligence	
Black	depth, sophistication, death, mourning, drama, gloom, magic, evil, disaster, fear, formality, piracy, wickedness	
White	enlightenment, healing, truth, purity, innocence, light, cleanliness, surrender, cover-up, fright, death	
Aqua and Turquoise	motivation, dynamism, imagination, intensity	
Green	growth, abundance, vitality, prosperity, achievement, fertility, balance, harmony, peace, hope, jealousy, inexperience, gardening	
Royal Blue	joy, loyalty	
Blue	peace, sincerity, truth, affection, tranquility, heavens, honesty, loyalty, reliability, quality, masculinity, improper language, sadness, coolness, philosophy	

Indigo	knowledge, power, integrity, pause, meditation, sophistication	
Purple	spirituality, passion, rage, vision, creativity, pomp, royalty	
Lavender	romance, fantasy, femininity	
Pink	friendship, femininity, caring, gentleness, compassion, faithfulness, health, optimism	
Magenta	imagination, innovation, energy	

color in information design

uses of color

Whatever your use for color, the color must have an integral role in telling the story you want told. Except for artwork on an attention-grabbing poster, for example, the color used should provide more meaning or direct the eye to more discovery. When it becomes "only about the color," your story is likely to be obscured. Not that color isn't meant to provide beauty—it is! A presentation of black and white overheads will probably not elicit the same reaction as a presentation in color. But color requires more care and thought, since there is a fine line between colorful and gaudy. Color can provide rich levels of information. For example, maps that depict water's depth or mountains' height use color as a measurement.

Edward Tufte lists the four fundamental uses of color:

1 **measurement**, as on a map

2 **label**

3 **representation of reality** (rivers on a map are blue, parks are green)

4 **decoration**

In three of these cases, color is working on two levels because it adds beauty as it represents, provides a measurement, or establishes a label.

choice of color

The choices one makes in choosing color are clarified by Tufte's list of the rules for the use of color in maps defined by the cartographer, Eduard Imhoff, in *Cartographic Relief Presentation*. Three of these rules have universal application:

1   Bright or strong colors are "unbearable" when used in large amounts. Bright, extreme colors are most attractive when used in small amounts on a muted background.

2   Light, bright colors placed next to one another in large amounts yield "unpleasant" results.

3   Muted colors, mixed with gray, provide the best background.

4   Two large fields of adjacent color cannot look unified. Unity is best maintained when a large field of color contains some spots of adjacent color, like tan islands in a sea of blue and tan land color with a sprinkling of lakes and rivers. This last rule is specific to maps and information design, since many artists successfully violate it.

Document Appearance

The form is that part of the world over which we have control... The context is that part of the world which puts demands on this form; anything in the world that makes demands of the form is context. Fitness is a relation of mutual acceptability between these two.

Christopher Alexander

paper

Paper is a significant part of the cost of any document and is an important component of the final look. Using a paper you know well will save headaches. Printers are generous with samples that you can try out. You may decide to combine different types of paper in one piece for variety and interest, keeping in mind the impact each kind of paper will have upon your message. Consult with the printer and have him or her show you printed examples. For example, parchment with a deckled (rough, torn-looking) edge connotes an antique feeling, so you might not choose it for a piece intended to look ultramodern. There are important paper properties to consider.

color

Black type is most easily read against a soft, neutral, or yellowish white. Colors reproduce most accurately on neutral white paper. Paper with a mottled appearance can make text difficult to read.

opacity

How much does printing show through from the opposite side of the sheet or the next sheet? Parchment, for example, has a beautiful, translucent look, but you might want each sheet in a document to

---

stand alone without distraction from succeeding sheets; consider a more opaque paper.

finish

The finish of a paper is its relative smoothness. Examples of finishes, in order of increasing smoothness, include antique, eggshell, vellum. The more absorbent the paper, the lower the printed contrasts will be. Glossier papers allow more vivid colors and starker contrast. If your paper needs to stand up to lots of handling, such as a presentation flip-folio that you will use over and over, ask a printer for a synthetic stock.

thickness

Measured in thousandths of an inch, the bulk or thickness of papers can range widely in pages per inch of a given weight.

grain

Machine-made paper has a grain, just as wood does. The grain of a piece of paper is in the machine direction—the direction paper is run through the papermaking machine. This direction of fibers within paper will affect the way paper folds. Try to fold a piece of paper across the grain and notice the bumps and cracks in the fold. Direction will also affect the way paper lies within a book or catalog. If the bound edge is not parallel to the grain, pages will not lie flat and will not turn easily.

weight

The weight, in pounds per ream (500 sheets) of paper for a given grade of paper is often the way we refer to paper. You have heard of 20 lb. bond or 70 lb. coated paper. But you will have to check on more than weight when purchasing, since prices are usually based on size as well. For a brochure or a cover, you will be directed to 60 to 100 lb. paper, since its opacity is critically important. Standard papers you might use for a résumé, for example, can range from 20 to 70 lb.

size

There are some different considerations with respect to size:
When and where will the document be read? If it's an office reference and a binder might work just fine, use standard 8.5-x-11-inch
paper. If you want to produce a small brochure that can fold into
pocket size, you might want to have a special size cut. Experiment
first.

What is the content? Are there large graphics or tables? How will it
be bound and distributed? Does it need to be mailed, either in an
envelope or as a self-mailer?

stationery

Small businesses have the same needs for good-quality stationery that larger ones do. If you are in a small business, your stationery will be judged against the businesses with big budgets behind them. Well, don't worry too much. Money doesn't ensure excellence in design or taste.

The same rules obtain for designing your own letterhead, card, invoices, or notepaper as for the written documents described here. The design must stand on its own and convey the message you want conveyed. Do you think you need a logo? Consider all the reasons you think so, and consider the consequences of not having one. If the answer is logo, hire a graphic designer to help you. Think of all the logos that offer instant recognition: everyone knows the Nike *swoosh,* or the McDonald's arches. If you want to communicate who you are, your corporate identity, in a graphic and instantaneous way, get a professional to help. Or if you want a special effect, like embossing, you will need the services of your printer. If all you need is some letterhead and envelopes with all the pertinent information preprinted, you can prepare them yourself without having to be a desktop publishing wizard.

identity in general

Everyone in business tries to establish an identity: a unique and consistent visual message. That identity starts with the name. If your business already has a name, creating an identity system will establish the image you want to project. However, your business's name narrows the range of images a bit. Brainstorm the words and concepts that relate to your business. Which do you want to emphasize?

If your business is new and has no name, you have the freedom to create one (or to hire a public relations/design firm to help you create a name). What do you want people to remember? Do you work with a global audience? What name works for all aspects of your business? Think about the growth and change your business will experience; can the name you select tolerate that evolution? So many businesses carry a name that was trendy once, but outdated now. Think about potentially selling your business; if your business carries your own name, will you be able to part with it? I thought about this last point, in particular, when creating my own business's name. I doubt I will sell it, but I would despair of ever selling or closing a business with my name on it. So I chose words that described my hope for the work I'd be doing. The name is *lumin guild*; *lumin* is intended to connote light or illumination. The word *guild* was chosen to send a message that a group of related, connected practitioners can exchange ideas here. Well, it was my attempt at metaphor, which is usually a good idea in naming. Would a PR firm have come up with something much better? Absolutely! But I created it in a very efficient ten minutes.

It is true that the style of your identity pieces will send the message, convey the image. Primary colors and blocky characters will send the message that your business is related to children, for example. Whatever you do to express your identity, the most important considerations, once the message is determined, are clarity, consistency, and uniqueness. Each element of your identity system, from letterhead to business card, should be similar to every other element, with a bit of variation to make it interesting.

letterhead

With letterhead, the impression that typeface, size, and color convey can have a significant impact on your business. Look at examples of letterhead in your mail, in design books at the library, anywhere you can, to get an idea of what you like and don't like. Keep in mind the function of your letterhead: to let recipients know from whom and where the communication is coming and how to reach you! Keeping that function in mind, allow your letterhead to reflect your personality and project an image for your business.

Typically, the business name and address information is printed at the top of letterhead, and names of individuals are printed at the side or bottom. You can change this model to suit your needs, but if you want to make a bold statement, get help from a graphic designer. Be sure that the printed elements will line up properly with your conent. There is no need to make this look like a newspaper headline! Set the name and address in a reasonable size font, close to the size of your body text. If you have a logo separate from the name, feature it. The options are endless: you can line up the address in a block or string it out as a line. Add rules and borders, or not.

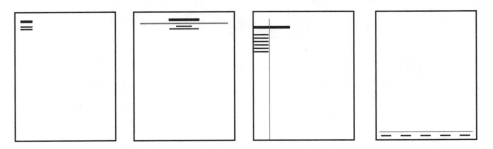

Test your designs by creating a letter in your usual style, without any of the letterhead elements, and printing it on an acetate (clear sheet used for overhead projection) to lay over your mock-ups. It's best to evaluate the letterhead when it's doing its job.

Once you've mocked it up, you can go to a printer for the final run. It is handy to be able to pop letterhead into the personal printer. It is best to have all of your stationery printed at one time to be absolutely sure of a consistent finished product. If you're not ready for the expense of printing letterhead (and I believe cards are more important, if you must choose), you can set up a template file in your word processing application and use the "save as" option for each letter you write. In this way you do have the option to refine the design before committing to a printed version, but do not make so many changes that your customers have trouble recognizing you from letter to letter.

the paper

Paper quality and color also send a message. Check papers with several printers, and even take samples (they're happy to help) to test on your equipment. Bumpy-surfaced papers might not produce a clean letter in your printer. A larger paper stock will be more costly than a standard size stock. Do try mailing a printed letter to yourself. Sounds silly, but if you've ever received a letter or brochure with ink smudged on facing sheets or cracked in folds, you *know* how much that impressed you! Make sure that the paper you choose offers sufficient contrast with the printed word. If you choose a darker stock, you will need to use a heavy typeface; that's fine if a heavy typeface fits your company's personality. Printers can advise you about all of these factors, but it's up to you to make sure it's going to succeed.

business cards

Business cards are a special case, and I have many biases. Cards are the most important stationery item you have because they are the most exposed. These are only my opinions, but here's what I would recommend:

Use a printer for production. Cards produced on a personal printer are rarely attractive. OK, some are. There are exceptions. But a printer can do it faster and better.

Keep them the standard size of 3.5-by-2 inches. Many people file them in a Rolodex-style system or at least in a wallet. You want your card to be easy to store.

Avoid a folded card. I've only seen one that was effective and a graphic designer created it. Key information is hidden within the fold, and the card takes up twice the space in file or wallet. (Don't tell anyone, but I tear off the part without key information.)

Landscape orientation is the standard, because that's how cards are stored and because of the available space for longer lines of type. If you have a really great design in a portrait orientation, just be aware that you may make it a little bit harder for your customer to find you in her card Rolodex.

White space! Have some. Good grief, I've been handed cards smothered in text. Offer some visual relief with some open space.

A dark card can be dramatic, but there are drawbacks. Recently someone gave me his black card with white and colored writing. OK, but I left my neon pink pen at home, so now how do I note anything on the card?

Novelty stock, such as translucent, is beautiful. I use one. But be careful of using a stock that is too translucent. People like to make notes on cards—for example, to remind themselves of where and when they met you. Don't make it hard for them to reach you again. Bear in mind, also, the message a translucent stock might send. If your company needs to shout "solid!" or "substantial!" or even "reliable," you might want to use more conventional paper. (I am reliable! But I want to convey a message about light.)

Coated cards may be hard to write on. Plus, these cards can curl. If you're set on a coated card because you want to include a photograph or intricate graphic (the applications to which coated cards are well suited), ask the printer to give you some sample stock.

Keep the graphics minimal. If you want a good graphic, pay to have one created and use it throughout your entire complement of stationery items. But be SURE to keep the graphic and printed areas separate, unless the writing can be read clearly. If it's hard to read, it probably won't be.

Keep the body type small and clear. Your company name or your name can be large, but set information like addresses and fax numbers small. I've received a few very amateurish cards set in large type. Be careful. Unless you are artistic, overall use of large type is rarely attractive. Use a typeface that is easy to read. Get a few opinions. I've received cards that were unreadable and too much effort to bother with.

Go ahead and use the back. But don't feel you have to do it. The back might be the place to add a key piece of information about your business, if it can be done in a few words. This is not the place to add a small-type version of your mission, vision, and goal statements. Remember, you need a little white space for eye relief and notes.

Stay with conservative colors in paper and ink unless you've had help from a designer or you've tested the look on many people who won't just tell you what you want to hear.

And, this has nothing to do with information design, but rather concerns etiquette. Don't hand your card to someone who hasn't requested it! Guess what he is going to do with it as soon as you're out of sight. Save them for the people who will treasure your shining gems of brilliant design and execution.

invoices

Your invoices should resemble other items in the range of stationery you use, from paper to typeface to logo. There are many business software applications that will set up your invoices for you. Customize the default invoice so that you can keep all of your paper output looking consistent, if you don't have printed letterhead. If you do not use a billing package, set up a template in your spreadsheet application (or use one of the ready-made templates offered) and be sure you have all of the elements covered.

notepaper

Notepaper and compliment slips are scaled-down versions of letterhead, with a less formal look. Notepaper can be of a size you find most useful. At minimum, you should include your name, with or without your company name. This is a good approach if most of your communications are to people who know you well, or who work within your organization. Include your address, phone number, and email address in business notepaper to give recipients who are not as likely to have your information right at their fingertips.

compliments slips

Compliments slips are often overlooked and present a polished image. Do you ever ship items to customers? A compliments slip is often one-third the size of an 8.5-x-11 paper or smaller, with the company name, logo, and address information. Somewhere away from the address, have a space where you can handwrite a short message. This is an informal communication, but it says you thought enough of the recipient to include a message. Even if you handwrite nothing (most often the message is printed), the effect is more personal. You can use a postcard stock and get two uses out of the same printed material.

Experiment by creating a mock-up of stationery or business cards for a famous fictional or historic character: Harry Houdini, James Bond, Florence Nightingale, whoever. Have some fun with it! If you create it in your word processing application, pull in some clip art. Think about the message you think your "client" wants to convey as you evaluate your masterpiece.

document sequence

That long document you've been working on is complete. Now all the text and related pieces need assembling. Ever wonder what the rules were for the sequence of contents for a document? Someone at Xerox has answered the question for you. If you need detailed information for a larger work, consult Adrian Wilson's *Design of Books*. These are rules, but you needn't feel that you need to follow every one to the letter. It helps to know the standards and then decide what is best for your document. You should know that even the authorities disagree here and there about the order of some elements.

Generally, documents are broken into three sections, consisting of front matter, subject matter and back matter. Many books, and most documents smaller than a book, do not have all the elements listed. This is simply the order of possible elements you will typically find. The front matter, or preliminaries, with the lowercase Roman numerals for page numbers starting with the foreword, should be in the following order:

front matter

Item	Description	Left/ Right
Blank leaves		
Half title	This is more correctly called the "bastard title" but frankly, half title is a nicer name. This page precedes the actual title page, serving as a protection page. Modern works commonly omit this element.	R
Advertising card	A list of the author's works, which can face the title page or may be placed on the back of a frontispiece.	L or R
Frontispiece	A pictorial page often facing the title page, it should be unified with the title page.	L
Title page	Contains title, author, version, publisher.	R
Copyright page	Legal information, such as publisher, address, any trademarks or notices, may appear sunk to the level of the lowest line on the title page and set in small type. Other elements, such as advertising card or dedication, may be combined with the copyright page.	L
Dedication	Usually a brief statement on a left page, but it can be combined with copyright.	L or R
Table of contents	Always begins on a right page, guides readers to major chapters and sections, may include list of figures and tables.	R

Illustration list	Contains captions, credits, locations. If the detail is significant, it can be placed at the back of the book.	L or R
Abbreviations	List of abbreviations used in the text.	L or R
Quotations	These may appear at the beginning of a part of the book, following a major heading, or in front.	L or R
Foreword	Statement by someone other than the author, usually an authority in the field.	R
Preface	Brief, interesting information by the author, giving the reason for writing the document, including brief acknowledgments.	R
Acknowledgments	A separate part only if the are many people to acknowledge.	R
Introduction	Unnumbered, chapter-level element that gives an overview. Might outline key concepts and terminology, background, or methods of using the document. The introduction is considered a preliminary element if it is not written by the author.	R

The subject matter, with Arabic numbers for page numbers, should be in the following order:

subject matter

Item	Description	Left/ Right
Introduction	Unnumbered, chapter-level element that gives an overview. The introduction is considered a text element if it is written by the author.	R
Parts	Collection of chapters grouped by concept.	R
Chapters	Major block of information.	R
Sections	Subdivision of a chapter.	R
Text and graphics	Content.	L or R
Summary/ conclusion	Depending upon content, summary or conclusion may be a final chapter or may appear as part of the back matter.	R

The back matter, with alphanumerics (A-1, A-2) for page numbers, should be in the following order:

back matter

Item	Description	Left/ Right
(Summary/ conclusion)	See Subject Matter.	R
Appendices	Appendices are lengthy reference materials or important information.	R
Glossary	Defines important terminology used. Terms may appear in italics within the text.	R
Endnotes	Cite documents used in numerical order, divided by chapter. If a bibliography appears, endnotes need only use author/date.	R
Bibliography	Lists documents consulted in preparation of a document. May be a single list, divided by subject or type of document.	R
Index	Included terms, topics, concepts, titles, cross-references containing far more detail than the table of contents. Usually set in double columns in a single-column book. Smaller type size than body text. If long, breaks occur between letters of the alphabet.	R
Response/ order form	List of related publications may appear here with order information or form.	R
Colophon	Identifies the designer, typeface, paper, ink, printer, binding.	L or R

INFORMATION DESIGN DESK REFERENCE

covers

The cover of a document is the first thing your audience sees. If your audience consists of people within your organization, the cover need only describe clearly the content within, such as the title, the department, or author. If you want to add a graphic to the cover, think about the most important messages within the content and then consider the message that makes the best visual statement. A simple graphic that does not compete with the important cover information is best. If your document is for sale, the cover needs to attract attention while complementing the content. If you are counting on significant sales, or if you are writing to an important audience, hire a graphic designer whose work is known to you. It will be worth the investment.

Two versions of an extremely simple report cover are shown to illustrate how alignment can create a polished look. In the centered version, the eye isn't drawn particularly to any location, except the title, which is larger, bold, and capitalized. All of the information is grouped in the center of the page. The other version shows the right-justified title and description at the top left, and the left-justified author name and date at the bottom right. I've added the line (which would NOT appear on the actual cover!) simply to show the alignment of elements along a common vertical. That invisible line leads the reader's eye from the important element to supporting elements; it organizes the way the reader moves through the information.

What a difference alignment makes!

Don't center everything! It can end up looking chaotic. Instead, lead the reader's eye. We start reading at the top and scan down left to right.

binding

Long documents need to be placed into something that will keep pages in order, and documents that are expected to be around for a while should be bound in some way. The choices boil down to:

— Do I need the pages to lie flat?

— What does the binding cost?

— What image does the document need to project?

— How long does the document need to last?

— Will pages be added or removed at times?

— Can the inner margins accommodate the binding?

The last question points out the need to consider the binding style before the document is prepared. If you know you will be using a binding that doesn't lie flat or that eats up inner margin space, you'll set up your document margins accordingly.

Book binding, with multipage sheets, is best left to the pros. If you want to read an excellent summary of binding styles, consult Jan White's *Graphic Design for the Electronic Age*. Binding single sheets can be done very simply, from stapling to a three-ring binder.

which binding is best?

For an example, I checked with Kinko's about the cost of different binding systems and found that there is no difference in price among the different styles listed here. Kinko's prices for binding are determined by the cover stock used and volume; the type of binding makes no difference to the cost. So, once you've decided you'll pay for a binding, you need only decide about other factors, such as looks and ease of use.

which binding is best?

Binding	Lies flat?	Turn pages easily?	Image	Add or remove pages?	Durability
Coil Continuous coil of plastic	Yes, folds back on itself	Yes	Good, eats up least inner margin	Only by replacing coil	Good
Comb Curled comb of wide plastic teeth	Yes, with up to 450 pages	Somewhat easily but pages can get stuck in position	Good, but binding is prominent when booklet is open	Somewhat easy	OK—comb can become brittle and pages tear out easily
Wire Metal spiral of wire	Yes	Yes	Good, eats up least inner margin	Yes, with the right equipment	Good
Tape Cloth tape	No	Yes	Good, but plan a larger inner margin	No	Strong, but the adhesive may give out in time
Velo Thin plastic strip forms edge	No	Yes	Good, but plan a larger inner margin	No	Good
Stapled seam Used with long, folded pages	No	Yes	Fair, used for newsletters and catalogs	No	Fair
Three-ring binder	Yes	No	Fair	Yes, easily	Good, pages may tear out

Incorporating
Graphic Elements

To envision information—and what bright and splendid visions can result—is to work at the intersection of image, word, number, art. The instruments are those of writing and typography, of managing larger data sets and statistical analysis, of line and layout and color. And the standards of quality are those derived from visual principles that tell us how to put the right mark in the right place.

Edward R. Tufte

when to use a graphic

When do you need a graphic? Some would claim that a graphic is legitimately an attention-getting device, or a mere relief from text. If getting attention is your main purpose, as in a poster, go for it. But for most documents, why spend the time to create and include something that has no role in informing your reader? Every element should have a role and be integrated within the content.

Journalism professor Eric Meyer recommends thinking about the answers to the five W's and two H's that news people consider. Is one of the questions of critical importance in explaining the story? That could be the clue that a graphic would serve to increase the explanatory power of your document. What are some examples of those W's and H's?

Who:	A bio, picture
What:	Key points
When:	Time line, schedule, chronology, clock
Where:	Map, picture
Why:	Comparison of various approaches, pros and cons
How:	A blueprint, diagram, instructions
How much:	Bar charts, graphs, pie charts

Certainly a graphic can tell more than one aspect of the story: you might combine a time line (When) and a bar chart (How much) to show annual amounts of grant funding for your agency during the terms of its three CEOs (Who). In this way, your illustration offers not only an additional perspective but communicates the information quickly, in a way that only a graphic can.

There are only a few exercises in this section on graphic elements. I included none in the sections on tables and charts, but I urge you to experiment, using a different approach from your usual one.

photo or illustration?

You are creating a mood with any artwork, a mood that may make it worthwhile to spend the money for color photography or for an illustration. Whatever you use, credit your source. Even clip art can be copyrighted and unusable for mass distribution. So, which to use?

— If your message is abstract, an idea rather than a thing, an illustration will work best. Plus, you can manipulate the message with an illustration more easily than with a photo.

— Use a photograph when you must describe a real thing. A photograph adds credibility because it shows the viewer the closest possible approximation of reality. Because they depict reality of a moment frozen in time, photographs have the capacity to stir emotions. If you do use a photograph, be sure to orient it properly. People pictured should face the content, rather than gaze off the page. You want to lead readers to your message by creating a path for their eyes.

Oh, well. You get the idea...

cropping photographs

Just a few words about incorporating photos into your creation: Often, a photograph will need some cropping, depending upon what you want to depict, but first you need to start with a good photograph. If you have a photo of a dog jumping a hurdle in an agility competition, you might want to focus in on the airborne dog. But if you want to show what an agility course looks like, you will need to keep the dog in the context of the course. Showing the happy airborne dog appearing to enjoy the experience of flight might interest dog owners in your new agility course. Showing the entire course, and the dog jumping a hurdle within it, could interest spectators in coming to an agility event. When possible, take out elements that will distract from your objective. Ideally we would start with a photograph lacking in distracting elements, but we don't always have the ideal photo.

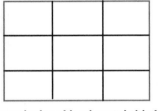

vertical and horizontal thirds

The rule of thirds is helpful in cropping photos. Divide the image (mentally!) into horizontal thirds. If your image has a horizon line, place this line one third of the way from the top or bottom. Or, divide the image again into vertical thirds, and place the focal point of your image at one of the four intersections of the four lines. For example, you have a photo of a speaker (your boss), taken from one side of the auditorium, holding an audience spellbound, and you want to include it in the department newsletter. Crop the photo to place her at one of the intersection points, and show some of the audience around her.

An aside about centering the subject. I would never say that centered arrangements never work. You might have a very effective photo of a situation with the backs of audience members' heads (silhouetted, I hope) and the speaker's head, centered, facing the audience.

Irrespective of centering or not centering the subject, the feeling certainly changes in this case. In the same situation a photo taken from within the audience would give the viewer the feeling of being an audience member, while the other photo provides the perspective of an uninvolved third party.

Before you actually crop a photograph, be sure to preview it. With an actual photograph, using L-shaped pieces of mat board like those you see in the frame shop will give you an instant idea of the final look. Never cut a photo with scissors! If you're sending the publication to a printer, get the printer to show you how to make crop marks on a tissue overlay, if that's what he requires. For digital images, cropping is done easily with the software tools packaged along with the photos. (The cropping tool is often depicted as two L-shapes.) With digital images, cropping is limited by resolution. Resolution will determine how much you can enlarge a specific portion of an image.

crop tool

This exercise will give you some practice in cropping and will sharpen your future photographic technique. Look at a recent batch of your own photographs and select a few that you think could be improved. Create two L-shapes out of paper or cardboard, larger than the size of your photos. (They should be at least two inches in width, and each extension of the L should be six to eight inches in length.) Look at different ways to crop the photos to bring out the focal point.

Next time you are out shooting photos for a project, think about what will help make them more compelling. Sometimes just getting closer to the subject is all that is necessary. Or, if the subject must be shown in context, be sure the subject's position somehow describes his relationship to that context.

the power of graphics

You're given a map or written directions to a friend's house. Which are you better able to use? Depends on the quality, of course. Each uses, primarily, one side of the brain. If you combine map and written directions, the effect is much more powerful and accommodates both the visual and the verbal types. A graphic has the capacity to be much more engaging and to convey more information.

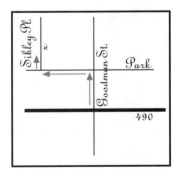

Directions to our house:
490 to Goodman exit.
Then follow Goodman to Park
and take a left.
Turn right at Sibley Place.
Fourth house on right.
Park in back.
15 Sibley Place.

Or, take an example from project management. What if I told you that it costs one hundred times more to correct errors in the maintenance phase of a project than it does if the errors are caught in the requirements definition phase? You might say, "So what?" But if I

---

showed you the graphic below you might be impressed with the dramatic rise in costs. Better yet, you will probably be more likely to recall the information later if you've seen the graphic.

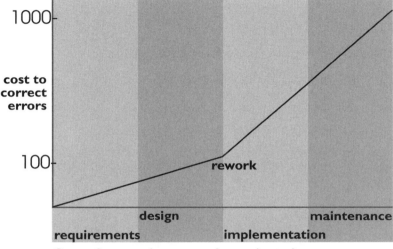

Cost of correcting errors by project phase

ACTIVITY: If you've ever tried mind-mapping, you have already done this exercise to some extent. Try to create a simple mind-map of a talk you will give, a report you will write or some other assignment. Take a sheet of paper and write in the center the main word or concept of the talk or report, then surround that central item with the four or five most important ideas you want to convey. Do it once, using words, to get your ideas down quickly. Then start again and try to reduce the number of words and use as many pictures or symbols as you can.

making your graphic communicate

Journalists have traditionally used the inverted pyramid technique. Start with the main point and then offer secondary points and supporting detail. Graphics and text can be employed in the process. But graphics will get more attention and will be processed more quickly than text, and readers will not always want to spend time scouring for meaning.

Make sure your main points stand out in the largest and darkest type, while secondary points use smaller type. Use boldface for the occasional important word in a secondary point. The journalists' term "glance box" is telling. Readers should be able to gather some meaning at a glance, since they will often skim, rather than peruse carefully. One main focal point is most effective.

Your reader needs clarity and simplicity, not because he or she is simple, but because there is no time for nonsense. Cluttering your graphic with needless decoration will only detract from your message. Resist the temptation to use every gismo, bell, or whistle offered by spreadsheet charting software, for example. Sure, these applications will allow you to create 3-D extravaganzas from your simple data set. But adding a content-empty dimension will confuse your reader.

Worse, it will reduce your credibility as a reliable source of information. The goal is to make the complex clear, not vice versa.

So, we know we have to organize the information, make it stand out, and keep it simple. Keeping a chart simple often includes leaving out the key or legend: you know, the box in the corner that tells you what all the colors mean. The colors in a graphic will have the most meaning incorporated into the explanation within the graphic. Keys are justified if the colors used have meaning. Then, a key to describe the use of blue for rain and white for snow on a weather map would make sense. If your graphic can't be read without lots of captioning and pointers, you probably need to do more work on it.

Don't mistake keeping the presentation simple for eliminating detail. In eliminating details you assume the worst about your reader. She needs to be able to see all the relevant information, but to see it clearly—that's the trick. Information design guru Edward Tufte advises careful inclusion of all relevant detail to permit the viewer to discern the needed facts. He abhors presentations of data light on detail and heavy on decoration, calling these "chart-junk." Tufte is probably the most highly regarded author on information design; his books are insightful, enjoyable reading, and as hard to put down as a good novel for those of us interested in the topic!

Look around you and find some graphics to critique. You probably receive flyers with graphic elements, or you can page through the newspaper or the yellow pages, as I did. Often they are excessively ornamented, or unclear. What would you do differently? Make a photocopy of one you'd like to redesign. Take it apart and put the components back together in a more effective presentation.

tables

In Japan, one has many occasions to use trains for transportation. I remember marveling at the layout of the schedules on the walls of the train stations. Only those data elements absolutely needed were there, and no extraneous or confusing detail was allowed in. (I reproduced an example of this schedule on page 24 in the section "Organizing Information.") The schedules were a wonderful example of the complex made clear—not simple, clear. My hosts compared the charts' spare presentation of the facts to the lack of any extra space in Japan. Every inch counts. Whatever the reason, I was impressed. They were clear, easy to read, and gave all the needed detail. From afar, a timetable resembles a frequency distribution, with the peak run times showing a longer row of numbers. Plus, the leading number of the hour is shown only once, at the side. Brilliant! Not repeating that number over and over saves the eye the work of sorting through to get to the needed detail. A few months after my return I happened to open Edward Tufte's book *Envisioning Information*. The elegant timetables from the Japanese railways are depicted several times in that text.

Tables can convey a great deal of meaning in a concise format, often much more clearly than prose. They get a reader's attention, simply because they are different from the rest of the document. Use a table when every detail is important and must be included and, as a result, a chart or graph would be misleading. If some details are more important or provide keys to understanding, highlight them. And hone it down to the most essential elements.

deciding to use a table (matrix)

Tables, with their rows and columns of information, can convey the message far more concisely than narrative description. Unfortunately, tables are often used poorly. Often a chart will say it better if you want to emphasize a particular aspect of a set of data. You need to ask yourself some questions if you are unsure whether or not a table is the way to present your information. If you can answer yes to at least some of these questions, you should be able to use a table well:

— Are **short text descriptions** for a number of supporting details needed?

— Do you need to show **precise values** of the data set?

— Do you wish to show a set of statistics in which **each item has fairly equal importance**?

— Do you want to **highlight a few important details** amongst surrounding detail?

— Would a simple **chart or graph hide too much of the information** you want the reader to know, such as exact values or numbers?

— Are you creating a rapid **reference tool** (like a mileage chart, for example)

— Do you need to **analyze a set of data** by sorting or ranking?

— Do you need to **make comparisons** and **show relationships** among data?

table format

Use a clear typeface and keep it as large as possible. Tables are commonly set in smaller type, but it is OK to keep the type the same size as the text. Titles should be larger and in boldface. Don't use all caps in titles, particularly if they require more than one word, and do use downstyle to keep them readable. If you keep with convention, you will place the headings in the center of the cell. I usually place them flush left, as in the sample table shown on page 148. It's easier to read since items appear in predictable locations.

Tables offer visual relief from the gray matter (text) on the page and do not necessarily need to match the column width of text. Nor do you need to place **boxes** around every cell: you've seen gray screens on alternate lines that permit ease of reading in long tables. The IRS uses that technique in tax tables, though not in a subtle or beautiful way. Go ahead and add a small splash of color as a horizontal rule, top and bottom for visual variety. You don't need to include vertical lines; given enough space between the columns, the eye will perceive the columns without them, and lines can cause the reader's eye to stop unnecessarily or to focus on the structure rather than on the content. Check out the table autoformat in your word-processing program. While many of the templates are garish and confusion-producing, a few of the options are reasonably simple and will save you some time.

Headings contain the variable information and should be kept as compact as possible. If you must have multiword headings, stack the words to keep the columns as narrow as possible, and abbreviate when you can. We also read left to right in tables, and too much space will make the eye wander.

Tables can compress quite a bit of meaning into a quick read. The information in the following table could be stated in a paragraph, but it is much faster for the reader to view the matrix, with its intersections of data. In addition, the schools with the highest numbers of scholarship winners are emphasized, making it even faster for the reader to get the most meaning out of the information in the shortest possible time. Note that a lack of data for a cell is signaled with a dash to let the reader knows it was left blank intentionally.

Scholastic Awards—2002

	Fremont High	Los Altos High	Sunnyvale High	Mountain View High
State Scholarships	82	75	90	88
National Merit Scholarships	—	8	9	4
NHS Members	245	212	306	227
Other Scholarships	126	141	189	193

charts and graphs

Charts and graphs are best used to summarize statistical and quantitative data in a visual manner. Most of us won't remember any amount of numerical data, but if you depict the same data symbolically in a chart or graph, we can then absorb far more information in far less time. Charts are visual summaries of statistical data and quantitative relationships. If you will be making frequent use of charts or graphs in your work, do refer to a detailed reference work like Eric Meyer's *Designing Infographics*. Most of us just want some of the keys to read-able and accurate charts:

Keep the data set clear without sacrificing important detail. If the data have many dimensions, you might need an additional chart to make the presentation clear. You must avoid confusion, which Tufte says is a failure of design, not the fault of complexity. In fact, Tufte would argue for the inclusion of detail to avoid ambiguity and to keep content rich. Further, he argues that the simplification of data can be perceived as an insult to your audience. Thus, we are back to the target audience analysis. The more sophisticated your audience, the more work you will have to do to arrange detail clearly.

Keep the look simple. Don't go crazy making it look colorful, or you will risk making your chart look less credible. Use only the minimum of grid marks and labels absolutely required to clarify the information. Heavy grid lines and table cells distract from the message—lighten them up, and the data they frame become the focus. The beauty of a chart is the information it conveys at a glance. Whenever possible, avoid legends, footnotes, or anything else that forces the reader to look somewhere other than the body of the chart for meaning.

Don't use all the features your spreadsheet program offers! All of the popular spreadsheet programs will produce charts for you; the trouble is that they produce charts that are far more complicated, much more elaborate than they need be, with useless legends and poor choices of color. You'll need to do some clean up. Too often we see three-dimensional bar charts that these programs produce. They're difficult to read because you cannot tell where the bar intersects the gridline.

Make sure it's accurate. The data must be right, and the depiction of the data must not distort.

bar charts

Bar charts are widely used because they are safest to use with many kinds of data. There is a tendency to decorate them because they are simple. You've seen the charts of car sales with little cars lined up in a row! That isn't wrong, but you can tell the story more simply. There is also a tendency to misuse bar charts. Here are some of the excellent guidelines offered by journalism professor Eric Meyer:

Keep the bars narrow. Charts look amateurish when the bars are wide.

Keep the space between bars half the width of a bar—unless you are stacking the bars to show a frequency diagram.

The scale must be higher than the largest value plotted.

Use a columnar bar chart to depict a trend with values based on an independent variable, such as change over time. If you used a line graph in the following "Seattle coffee consumption" example, the line would imply data samples that might not exist. If we only know a total amount of consumption for the entire year but do not have weekly or monthly data a line graph could mislead.

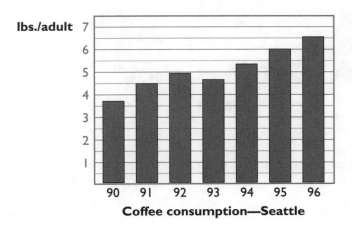

Use a horizontal bar chart to depict comparisons between discrete categories that are not equally related to an independent variable. In the subsequent chart "Cups of coffee per day," there is no depiction of a change from a previous point, as there is in the vertical bar chart "Coffee consumption," where we observe an upward trend. If we mix up the order of the names in the horizontal chart, it really makes no difference to our understanding. You could still see at a glance that Tim is quite a coffeeholic. If we were to mix up the years in the vertical chart of coffee consumption in Seattle, it would be difficult to assess the trend.

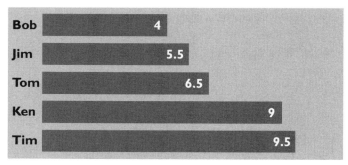

Cups of coffee per day

Keep the data labels from becoming a distraction: they should be close to the bars, or you can place the labels OR actual values inside. Do not place labels AND actual values inside the bars. It looks messy and confusing.

If you use a grid, you don't need value labels on each bar. The columnar bar chart has a grid: values are not labeled. The horizontal bar chart shown here has no grid: values are labeled. Simplify the presentation by eliminating redundant elements.

line graphs

Line graphs, such as the "cost of correcting errors by project phase" on page 142, show trend data well, also. Line and bar charts can be used interchangeably sometimes, but generally, when you plot discrete data readings in a line graph, the line drawn between the readings contains implied data. If you do not wish to imply such transitional information, use a bar chart. For example, you cannot use a line graph accurately to depict the numbers of cups of coffee Tim, Ken, Tom, Jim, and Bob drank. The data do not show a continuous series of measurements. Even measurements of a trend over time cannot be shown in a line graph if the fluctuations between the measurements shown are extreme. For example, a line graph of quarterly readings of a stock price that fluctuated over a range of 90 points each month would not show the story of the stock's volatility accurately. A bar chart would show that readings were taken quarterly (at a point in time), but would not imply any smooth transition from one reading to the next. Professor Meyer advises: if you are in doubt about which is right, use a bar chart.

high/low charts

Speaking of stocks, and many people like to, the high/low chart is an excellent tool, and it depicts the variation in the data. Spreadsheet programs create these easily, and they have a number of applications. Suppose I gave the same test to four different groups of people (A, B, C, D) with different skill levels. They score pretty well overall on a test with 8 questions. Only one group, C, seems to have scored a little bit lower, but the variation is greater in group B, with a few people scoring lower than any of those in group C. The little dot in the center of each vertical distribution line is the average of the scores.

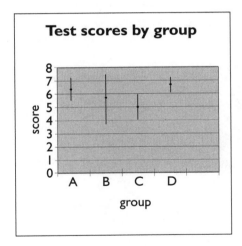

Most of us can gather a great deal of information from the "Test scores" chart, (which was created in Excel) much more quickly than would be possible from a read of the numbers upon which it is based, shown in the following table. In addition, it is best to provide the numbers as a reference. Some people will prefer to use the numeric data only and not use the chart at all. You might save yourself some work if you know your audience's preferences.

Group Score	A	B	C	D
Upper	7.15	7.48	5.89	7.15
Lower	5.51	3.81	4.11	6.11
Mean	6.33	5.64	5.00	6.63

filled fever charts

Filled fever charts should be used only if the data are additive. For example, the chart below shows donations to a charity by a specific source. It's appropriate to fill the area below the line because the quantities add up. A bar chart could also be used here. With discrete readings, like temperatures or stock prices, you would not fill the area below the line.

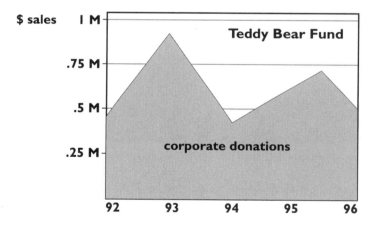

pie charts

Pie charts are best used for showing the proportion of components to one another.

Think you've seen just about enough pie charts? Yes, they are everywhere. I've seen an entire presentation with slide after slide of three-dimensional pie charts. It got old. Pie charts do depict proportions and percentages well, however. And it is easy to avoid legends since most data labels can be placed right in the pie. The trick to creating useful pie charts is, again, to keep them simple.

Spreadsheet software offers a host of complicated options. They allow you to create 3-D pie charts skewed, with a "visual effect," or with a second pie chart alongside to explain one section...the list goes on. You'll need to learn to set your own options! If you allow the software's automated features to add in useless frills, you put clarity at risk.

Keep the colors or shades of gray clear. Don't use lines and dots and other shadings for different slices, or you'll confuse your readers' eyes.

Use a pie chart when you have only a few segments to depict. If you're trying to divide the pie into fifteen slices, you should consider another way to show the data. Complex pie charts with many "slices" can be done well, but for the purpose of most informal presentations created with standard software applications, it is best to use a bar chart if you have many segments. Showing a large number of segments could be easy if there are a few large segments. The many additional segments could be represented as one small segment. Then the small segment could be broken out at the side as a list in table format or (I don't believe I'm writing this) another pie chart.

Make the most important information stand out. Explode the key element of the chart to emphasize its importance. Group segments together by shared attributes. For example, if your pie chart depicts sales by city in eight cities, you could group the cities around the chart by region and add in numeric subtotals for each region. The regional managers will be pleased, or perhaps displeased.

I used a drawing package, rather than a spreadsheet to create the simple pie chart about the school bond issue because it was a very simple data set and I wanted to customize the presentation. The spreadsheet chart automatically placed a legend (you can turn it off, of course) and gave me no easy choice of color. The pie chart gives a quick look at the vote on a school bond, since the sizes of the segments give the proportions of the votes. That's why I included the numbers of votes with the label, rather than the percentages, because the numbers are more informative. The numbers tell how many, not just a proportion, like 80 percent or 20 percent. Percentages could mask a low voter turnout; what if there were actually 400,000 people eligible to vote here? If information gathered in exit polls about opposition to the bond issue bears more discussion, you could add a breakout of reasons for opposition by percent.

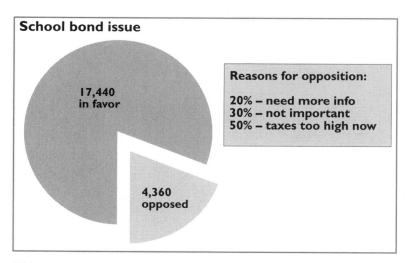

This chart was created in a drawing application.

The same chart, created very quickly in a spreadsheet program with easily selectable settings, is shown on page 157. I didn't get exactly what I wanted: the labels are not inside the pie chart; it included a distracting legend, and the pie is smaller than I'd like. I could have deleted the legend, but the presets did not allow the actual number of votes to appear with the word label, only a percentage. Also, the program set the colors of the pieces of pie to red and blue (they're gray here because the colors don't add any meaning so there's no sense spending extra on red and blue ink for this example!). With a little effort you can create a chart in a spreadsheet program that looks close to the way you want it to look. In this case I could not find an easy way to show the data labels next to the numbers.

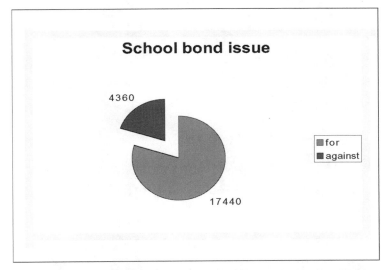

This rather ugly chart was created automatically by a spreadsheet.

schematic diagrams

Schematics are best used for depicting hierarchies and simplifying more complex systems, such as circuits or internal building systems.

We have frequent use for diagrams that show organizational hierarchies, family trees, or the internal structure of a building. We agree upon certain symbols and conventions to convey meaning: boxes under other boxes, connected by a line on an organization chart, describe supervisor/employee relationships. Keep them simple, and use subtle shading or callouts to emphasize important points. For example, shading and labels in the organization chart here show a department that has been downsized and the creation of new positions in marketing. We might gain some insight into the organization's direction as a result of the changes we see described in the chart.

ACME Industrials

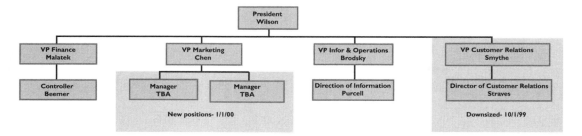

flow charts

Best used in brief form for critical tasks, or tasks performed infrequently, with significant negative consequences for errors.

A legacy of software developers, who seldom use it these days, the flow chart is often used to depict procedures and work flow. Flow charts were overused during the days of TQM (Total Quality Management). Long, complicated flow charts languished unread in large binders. Most procedures can be written in text, but if there are critically important decision points with resulting different actions, a flow chart works very well. Icons, shading, or symbols can be used to cue the reader to follow the correct path quickly. But use them sparingly. The following flow chart uses a maximum of icons; any more would be chaotic.

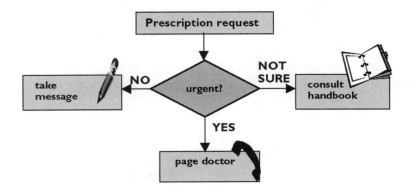

This flow chart is a *very* simplified phone triage procedure for the answering service of a physician group practice. Nothing is quite so black and white. The "gray areas," which I called "not sure," could be actually solved a number of ways, such as consulting a nurse or colleague, but I documented the first step to solving the quandary independently. New people would be instructed to verify!

I created similar charts for the most important procedures when I managed a busy clinical practice. If the procedure is performed often, only new people need access to the flow chart. But errors tend to occur with critical tasks performed infrequently. For instance, in a doctor's office a flow chart for post-needle-stick wound irrigation would be an excellent poster/job aid just above a utility sink.

Flow charts take too much time to be used to document every procedure in an operation. Yet I have seen this done. If you need to get a picture of the way an operation works, for example, try creating data flow diagrams, which will better depict dependencies between different components of an operation. Unless your colleagues work with flow charts frequently, you will find that many people do not understand the meanings of all of the different symbol shapes. The whole point of a chart is instant understanding, which is the reason for adding the clip art—it helps visual learners. If a key is needed to understand the meaning of the symbol shapes, the information you need to convey is less likely to reach its target.

Flow charts should be brief, if they are used at all. An outline of words-only can work just as easily for longer procedures. To give an example, the information in the previous flow chart can be represented quite clearly as follows:

Prescription request:
    Urgent?

Yes	➔	**Page doctor**
No	➔	Take message
Not sure	➔	Consult handbook or expert

If a long, detailed flow chart is unavoidable, it can work very well in the online environment where a click will take you to a subtask or to the next "page" of the chart. Software for creating flowcharts is very easy to learn.

diagrams

data flow diagrams

Best used for more detailed representation of the workings of an operation.

A more useful tool for representing entire business processes, as our work becomes increasingly more information intensive, is the data flow diagram. Since most organizational procedures involve transfer of information, the data flow diagram provides a simple view of the movement of information through an organization. There are only three symbols used:

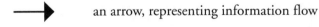 an arrow, representing information flow

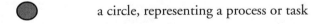 a circle, representing a process or task

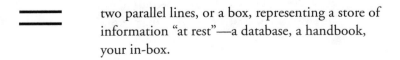 two parallel lines, or a box, representing a store of information "at rest"—a database, a handbook, your in-box.

Here's a data-flow diagram of the prescription request outlined and flow-charted above. The information is depicted as coming into the process. Next, the resulting data flow, based upon the incoming prescription request, is charted. Note that the process specifications, or rules, are referenced elsewhere.

The data-flow diagram highlights how processes are related by the movement of information. Procedures and rules are easily referenced but do not interrupt the diagram of information flow.

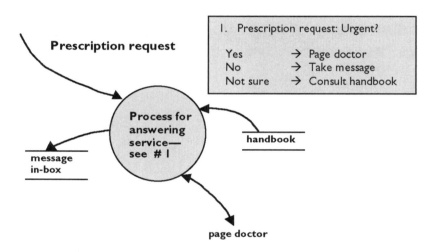

Notice the direction of the arrows. Messages are placed **in** the message in-box. Information is extracted **from** the handbook. The doctor is paged and must call back for a message. Other processes, such as updating the handbook or reading the messages, can be diagrammed, making the model a useful representation of the complement of information-based tasks that make up a small portion of an operation.

time lines

Best used when an account of dates and events is of primary importance.

Time lines help to keep a historical perspective on developments. You can list dates in a bulleted narrative form, but if you want a true time line, you need a consistent scale to mark the passing of time. You can switch scales in the middle if you note the change somehow (possibly with a color or type change) if more events need to be recorded in a section, but the new scale must be in even increments. Dates in the future can be included if they are clearly different from past dates with a new color or type. And every date can't be significant; don't emphasize the dates themselves. Emphasize only the most important events, either with bold print or, given the space, an illustration or graphic.

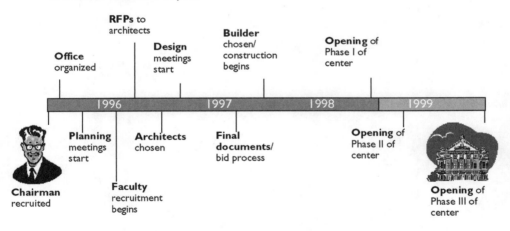

Research Center Project

It's always hard to decide what to include in a time line; the problem is usually what to leave out. With an interactive time line, on the Web or on a computer, you have the option to include supporting detail. A time line on a computer is fun for readers because they can choose to view only the high level information or choose to drill down to detail.

The Variety of
Documents

One can be sure that form always follows ingenuity.
Paul Rand

brochures

The brochure is a document most widely used, and most widely abused, by businesses. Do you need a brochure? I thought I did, created one, and later decided my portfolio of work was what prospective clients wanted to see. Fortunately for me, much of my work is on the Web. But for most businesses, if you are selling a product or service that needs information dissemination, paper brochures are still almost a requirement, since their purpose is usually to inform your audience and get them to contact you.

Brochures that support selling should do two things: give your audience the impression that they know your business well enough to give you a call, and tell your audience why you are unique or different. Brochures that inform need to be clear, above all. For example, an in-house vendor, like a training or printing department, does need to have a list of courses and services in order to market to the larger organization. Any brochure needs to be well designed enough to tell the reader what it is about in seconds and give the reader enough information to take action in a few minutes.

The marketing aspects of brochure production are best left to the experts who create corporate identity kits routinely. Read *The Com-*

plete Guide to Creating Successful Brochures listed in the reference section if you need specific information about the brochure-selling format. If you need serious marketing assistance, working with a public relations or advertising firm is probably unavoidable. Since my knowledge of marketing is quite thin, I will concentrate on the visual presentation here: the brochure as an image vehicle with implied messages, rather than a marketing vehicle.

Think about what it is your brochure is going to do for you. Do you need to describe a project or campaign? Or is the brochure going to serve an internal group, telling them about a department's staff and programs? Or do you need to tell (sell) about your organization, or to describe your products and services? This is where some marketing expertise is essential.

Whatever the purpose, all of the design elements must be unified, and the look of the document should be of a lasting nature. For a few years, broken, messy looking type was the rage, despite its illegibility. If your brochure will be around longer than a season, don't be tempted to use the latest-rage type designs or fad colors. Besides, why look like the rest when you can do something unexpected and stand out?

Before you begin designing the visual presentation and organizing the content, you need to answer some questions:

— Who is your target **audience** and what are their needs?

— What is your **objective**? One objective is plenty.

— How is the concept, service, or product **unique**?

— Do you want the brochure to function as a **self-mailer**?

— Will it sit in a store **rack,** or will you personally **hand it out**?

— What **action** do you want the reader to take after reading your brochure?

— Will more than one brochure (a **set of brochures,** similar in look) be needed to cover all the content?

target audience

You probably know your target audience's likes and dislikes better than anyone else. Let's say you run a landscape service, and your target audience primarily comprises busy families who want an attractive yard but have no time to achieve that goal. Designing a brochure that won't take long to read, but assures them of your expertise and cost-effectiveness, is important. A good cover photograph might show a beautiful landscape where children are playing. Inside, you might repeat some of the landscape details from the cover photograph, next to related copy. For example, if you want them to know you deliver only guaranteed-quality plantings, that beautiful ornamental tree in the front photograph would be a nice echo. If you want them to know you use only environmentally safe, nontoxic products, you could excerpt the child at play from the front photograph.

self-mailer brochures

If you will be mailing your brochure to your audience's home or business, take a draft to your local post office and get some advice. The post office has regulations about self-mailers: where to place the fold, size, closure materials (no staples!), and so on. Talk to them before you invest much time or any money.

Self-mailers can be attractive, but they take more effort. The closures commonly in use (sticky acetate circles or squares) can make or break the look. If your cover design is curved and flowing, go with a circle; if it's geometric, go with a square. Keep the color unobtrusive, or, if the brochure contains a strong color scheme, pick up a color or background hue with the closure.

Address labels on any mailing need to be applied straight, or the message received is that you are indifferent and that the recipient is merely one among thousands. If you can print the address directly on the brochure, the message you send is far better, since you (your printer) took the time to address each recipient's brochure neatly.

the display rack

Is your brochure likely to be sitting in a display rack where you hope it will be selected? The cover, the most important page in any brochure, must be eye-catching and descriptive. This is not the time to use stock brochure paper (not that I've seen evidence that there is ANY appropriate time to use stock brochure paper! There are exceptions, but most of it looks tacky). If you get no other artistic help, get some for the cover of a brochure that doesn't have you to lean on for distribution. It must cry out to be picked up by the people who need your product or service.

personal distribution

If you are likely to give your brochures to people you have spoken with on the phone, or to people you meet, the cover can be far subtler. The cover is still important, but it doesn't need to GRAB them as much.

the action you want from the reader

Start with the assumption that your reader will spend a small amount of time skimming your brochure. Then your brochure needs to tell a very brief story in the most compelling manner possible. Once again, the journalist's five W's—who, what, when, where, why—can be used effectively, to make sure you cover everything and that it's all there. The end of the story should invite an action. Do you want to receive a call? Make sure the phone number and email address are prominently displayed on the back cover, with all the other pertinent reader response information.

You might include a response card, separate from the brochure, but held within it. A response card might offer readers a free item or their score on the brief quiz it contains. It has to be worth the trouble for readers to fill out the name and address area on the card.

the visuals

Staid, boring visuals with a few headshots and some sappy clip art will not guarantee you great success. Talk with a friend or colleague about everything related to your concept, service, or product. Then think of analogies and metaphors. Do any **unexpected** visuals come to mind? The old Volkswagen ad campaigns were marvels of the unexpected. They made the ugliness and odd features of the cars into selling points; cars were seen floating, for example. They were different! That was good! I'm not saying, take this approach. But, you can feel free to come up with unusual photos or graphics. A good brainstorming technique would be to think of the most extreme example and scale it back a few notches in order to **match your visuals to your content** and to your target **audience's style.**

It's easy to say, "don't be boring." Try to visualize what it is your audience will want to see. Are you creating a brochure for your non-profit organization's venture into a new market? **Visualize the impression** you want to create. Your community rehabilitation center treats injuries, but there is increasing interest in treatment from students of the local music school. You now have the right staff to treat their specific types of repetitive stress injuries. Storyboard a series of photographs showing a student at the piano, then with a physical therapist, and finally on a concert stage. OK, that might be hokey. As an alternative, sketch a colorful CT-scan or MRI-looking scan of an arm, showing the hand holding a violin bow. Try another alternative, too, and test them on a few students. Do they prefer the happy ending up front? People do like to see solutions, such as the concert stage photo.

content

The message in a brochure must be **concentrated, distilled** to its essence. Short, clear statements with a specific message will hold attention far better than long-winded expository passages. And every aspect must lead the reader to the most important points, which may be benefits of a product, for example. Illustrations must be in harmony with copy and the most important words must stand out from the remainder of the copy. The brochure must be unified in all of its design elements.

I know I said this wasn't going to be about marketing, but before you write a word, think about the brochure from the perspective of your audience. What is in it for them? You will need to provide your reader with a **benefit.** Look for a book about writing effective marketing copy that will convince readers you can meet their needs.

Provide **unique information** and you will stand out from others. In fact, if you can't offer something unique and fresh in your brochure, you should stop and think before you spend a penny on it. Your brochure should be part of a larger strategy in which you deliver a powerful message about your subject. Upon reflection, you might find you need several brochures to cover different niches to which you wish to appeal with a clear, focused message. Or you might develop a brochure that approaches the subject from a totally unexpected point of view. Or you could simply tell people something they don't know.

A brochure shouldn't be one long, running narrative. People prefer looking at pictures, so break it up into **small chunks of information.** Give them short bursts of content, since chances are they're only going to glance at portions of your brochure.

Keep your **language conversational**; deliver facts rather than a strong sales pitch, slogans, clichés, and silly rhymes. Certainly a straight, unemotional approach, with the facts, figures, and supporting data, can do the job. Other approaches to the content can range from case history, to problem/solution, to testimonial, to before-and-after. Each is effective in presenting benefits to the reader because the source of the information is an objective third party.

Back to where I said the approach should be unemotional. That's the safe approach, but we all know you generally need to get an **emotional response to** move your audience to action. You can try to make them laugh, tug on their heartstrings, or fire them up about a cause. You'd better be a good writer and test your copy on several representatives of your audience. Frankly, I would hire a professional before I tried a significantly emotional selling technique. A good brochure will be costly anyway. Why take a risk with an emotional appeal if you aren't absolutely sure you can do it professionally?

Please, please avoid setting all of your sections of **copy** at different angles, as is often done. If you must, you can get away with doing some of this to emphasize a point, but it becomes tiresome for the reader to shift the page constantly. Visual variety, with pictures or graphics and white space, is expected. However, don't make the mistake, and I see this often, of placing important copy on top of graphic elements that render the copy unreadable. Don't waste your time and money only to risk not getting your message seen, or worse, putting your reader off. Aim for a harmonious relationship between the verbal and the visual.

Because brochures can be costly, either in time or money, make sure the brochure **content is not very susceptible to change.** Perhaps you will be printing your brochure from your home equipment. Even then, updating takes time. If you have a price list or a menu or anything else that you revise, consider making it a separate insert.

organizing techniques

Here are few more organizing techniques; several are from *The Complete Guide to Creating Successful Brochures*:

— Determine the **concept** to fit with your overall strategy.

— Establish a **visual hierarchy.**

— Give each **benefit its own section,** with its own supporting graphic or photo and copy.

— Use **checklists and bullet points.** They're faster to read if you keep the number of items low.

— Use **lead-ins** to guarantee the reader will turn the page.

— Use **quotes and testimonials** as callouts. They add credibility and visual relief.

— Use **captions** under photos. People read them first.

— Make sure **visuals are tied to the copy.**

> Look at any brochure and evaluate it according to the design principles starting on page 45. Does it work? Does the cover cry out for the brochure to be picked up and opened? Is the content clear and inviting enough to make you take the action desired by the authors?

postcards

Consider using a postcard for mailing your message to clients if you are an artist, photographer, architect, builder, designer, or anyone else who wants to get orders for work. Use the image side of the card for an excellent representation of one of your past works, and the back side can contain the basic information you have on your business card plus a very brief description of the pictured work. Add content telling the compelling (but very brief) story behind the picture, or describing the kind of work you do. You can use a postcard to announce an event, such as a seminar or grand opening. It's a positive way to keep in touch with your audience or clients; my dentist and veterinarian use very entertaining postcards to remind me of my appointments.

Postcards can be created with a blank side for a number of uses, if you can print the back yourself. They work to get a specific response, such as offering a discount or a free gift if the postcard is brought to your place of business—a common device for increasing traffic. You can use a postcard as you would a compliments slip, adding a personal note.

Your postcard should be appealing or attractive enough to interest your recipient into keeping it for a while.

newsletters

More and more newsletters are showing up in my email box. Many of them are ugly and uninviting; a few are very nicely done. I say, if you're going to take the time to do a newsletter, make it clear and attractive, or no one will read it. That goes for both paper and electronic types.

The first step in any endeavor, but particularly in a newsletter, is to ask why you are creating it. What is the unmet need that you will be fulfilling? Who will the audience be? Newsletters range from purely informative to downright marketing vehicles. They require quite a bit of effort, because they must be created on a periodic basis, and they must be distributed, often at a significant cost. Decide on the purpose of your newsletter before you proceed.

Once you know the purpose, think about the image your newsletter must project. Even if it is primarily an information piece, without graphics or color, the way it looks will affect how it is perceived and how it is distinguished from other newsletters.

when is simple OK?

Newsletters are really in the domain of desktop publishing, in which, if you intend to create a masterpiece, you need a more advanced reference. How do you know if you need to hire an outside resource or get more advanced training for your newsletter? How do you know when something simple to do is "enough?"

You need to outsource to an expert (or develop your own desktop-publishing expertise) if:

— your newsletter is a **marketing vehicle** to attract business, donors, or positive publicity

— your newsletter must convey an image of **prestige** and authority with respect to the content

— you are relying heavily on the **layout and graphics** to get a positive response

You can probably keep it simple if:

— someone is available with **time** and interest to create the document in a word-processing application

— you must, due to a **limited budget** for production

— your audience is very **interested in the content**—they seek it out in other places if you don't provide it to them

The last point is key. If you know you have an audience eager for the information, they probably will not be so concerned with a gorgeous layout and graphics.

I can give you an example. Many years ago I edited (translation: wrote articles, begged for articles, compiled, corrected, produced) a newsletter for a nonprofit group. We had a budget of zero for the entire endeavor; interested participants donated everything from paper to postage. The newsletter's purpose was to inform parents, teachers, and caregivers for chronically ill children of services, legislation, advocacy resources, and advances in care. Nothing of its kind existed, and recipients were happy to receive it. It was primarily text, with an occasional picture of a family or of children, and I used a word-processing application to create the format. Would I do things differently now? Oh, yes! I'd change everything from headline alignment to bullets and I'd add a guide to contents on the front. Here is a copy:

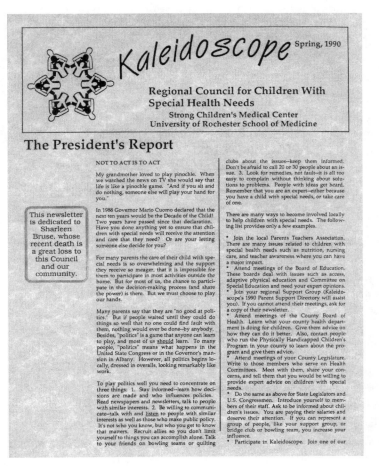

What do people like to see in newsletters? The same thing they like to see in newspapers and magazines. Stories about people, direct quotes (they draw the eye to the content), pictures, and any unique, helpful information. Keep the writing lively.

What kind of layout is best? Remember grids? You must decide on a grid to make the layout easy to follow. The back page can differ, since you will need to devote some space to addresses and postage. But the choice is up to you. The best thing to do is to look at samples and decide on the look you like best. Then experiment with the software you will be using.

How do you get it to look right? The word-processing application that came with your computer undoubtedly has a wizard function that will make it easy to format your newsletter. If not, the use of columns and sections within the document (that's how I did the one you see here) can achieve the look you want. You can insert picture or artwork files and set their properties to allow text to flow around them in various ways. Not that I'm never frustrated! You will do some hair pulling when you are fitting the copy to the pages.

How is copyfitting done? Start by having a pretty good word count for the publication. Then you can ask contributors for articles of, say, 600 to 800 words. Let them know you will be editing the content. Then paste the articles into the columns you have established and begin to add white space between articles and pictures or artwork. You can resize photos or artwork; larger when copy is scant, smaller when you can't spare an inch. Same goes for specialty content. In the Kaleidoscope newsletter shown, the inside lists resources for parents in a larger size font, since we wanted to draw them to this content. However, ads cannot be resized since they are purchased based upon proportion of the page. You must start with ads when creating your layout.

What guidelines exist for content? You don't have to create a rigid formula for content, but just as a grid helps with layout, a plan for content is very helpful when you make decisions about what gets included in each issue. A newsletter for a professional organization I joined recently devotes about 20 percent of its space to news about the organization, up to 50 percent of its space to articles and contributions by members, 10 percent of its space to a calendar of events, about 10 percent to advertising, and 10 percent to the mailing label location.

There is a danger to designating "Departments" for your newsletter if you can't find content for them from issue to issue. But do put content in predictable locations with each issue. For example, place those brief news stories that don't really merit a headline in a fairly consistent catchall location.

Provide guidance to the contents. Even if your newsletter is short, it's important for your reader to glance at a predictable location to find out "what's inside." This is where you sell the reader on turning the page or (sorry) scrolling down.

What are some sources of content? You could do a Web search, but for content that feels more personal or closer to home here are a few suggestions:

— Gain commitment from people in your organization to act as correspondents, contributing an article on a periodic basis.

— Request input, articles, and answers to readers' questions requiring expertise!

— Interview someone who is perceived as an expert or someone highly regarded. Quotes and pictures really draw the eye!

— Interview someone at a high level in your organization (if you are writing an organizational or department newsletter).

email newsletters

It's so easy to set up an email list that you might find yourself receiving many more e-newsletters than you can absorb. The email newsletter has some unique advantages: it's cheap and recipients can contribute simply by replying. If you want to send an e-newsletter these days, how you send it will depend on your audience's interest.

Create the e-newsletter in an HTML-based email message.
These can be very attractive to look at, but you'll need some technical and graphic know-how. You can always outsource the work on an HTML document for use on the Web or inside an email, if you have a budget. HTML emails are worth the effort if you are marketing high-priced or high-volume products and services. You will likely target people who can afford high-end equipment, so they won't be frustrated by the size of the email message. But don't use this approach just because you CAN. There are plenty of people who will not appreciate having to download large emails.

Send a link to the Web site with your newsletter. This is safer than a large email file from the standpoint of not making some recipients mad. The problem is, will they follow the link? You risk losing them with this approach because they're absorbed in reading emails and don't want to be pulled into another direction. So your message had better offer a pretty good incentive to go to the site.

Place a text-based newsletter in the body of the message. If you are marketing something they might not be so keen to receive without a little eye candy, this approach won't work, but it works just fine if the information is of great interest to your recipients. People want online newsletters with content they can't find anywhere else. They are great sources of information from experts in your field!

Guidance for a text-based newsletter. Since Web design is treated elsewhere, here's an example of about the best you can do with a text-based e-newsletter. By text-based, I mean the use of plain text (this used to be called ASCII text) with no bold or larger/smaller fonts. Your only options with this format are spaces between lines, upper and lower case letters, hyphens or small O's for dot points, numbers for items, and strings of underline characters for lines to separate sections. At this writing (undoubtedly it will change the day after this book is published) there are many email users who cannot read any other kind of message. Use the rich text or HTML format only if you know that the formatting lost when read into a plain text reader will not make a difference in the readability of your message.

The sample e-newsletter is a basic template showing the use of plain text characters for formatting. The look is not beautiful, but it is neat and consistent. You can copy it for each use.

```
ENEWS WEEKLY                              July 27
News and discussion about whatever
_____

                   SPOTLIGHT ON
      ------    -----   ---- - -- ----
            - --------- ------- - ----
_____

TODAY'S NEWS:
1. From the editor
2. What's up?
3. Questions for the pros
4. Resources
_____

1. FROM THE EDITOR
------    ----- ---- - -- ---- - --- ---
------ --------- - --------- ------ ---
--    -----  ---- - -- ----- ---


_____

2. WHAT'S UP
------    -----  ---- - -- ---- - ---
------ -------
--  - --------- ------- ----- ---- ---
-  -- ----- ----------


_____

3. QUESTIONS FOR THE PROS
o    ---- - -- ---- - ------- ---?
o    - --------- ------?
_____

Written by Anna Riley Wells, Director of Morale
Copyright 2001, luminaria
TO UNSUBSCRIBE- reply with remove in subject line
```

Your reader will be able to scroll to what he's looking for quickly with the table of contents at the top. Key content is set off in longer lines and short lines help to separate content sections. The apparently right-justified text is done with leading spaces; this works if you use Courier type.

spreadsheets

When you need to present a full spreadsheet, rather than a graph, you want the data to be clear and accessible. Rather than print a spreadsheet as is, with all of the distracting lines and labels, experiment with the auto-formats or create your own format. Emphasize the data you think important. Two sample spreadsheets are shown before and after formatting (done manually, rather than with the auto-format).

The way to be sure your spreadsheet is clear is to ask someone new to the information what stands out most. With luck and some good design, they'll point at exactly what you hope they notice most. Get rid of extraneous cell lines and emphasize the key numbers. Add a line above totals or add alternate lines of shading to make it easier to read across a long row of numbers. Spreadsheet programs, like word-processing software, offer the option of creating your own style to make the process more efficient, and to ensure they are consistent in appearance. As always, ask yourself if the formatting adds to clarity, or reduces it.

before format changes

	A	B	C	D	E	F	G
1							
2	**Problem Selection Matrix**						
3	*A decision aid for prioritizing issues*						
4							
5		Option	Option	Option	Option	Option	Option
6	Control	A	B	C	D	E	F
7	Little Great						
8	1 2 3 4 5						
9	Importance						
10	Little Great						
11	1 2 3 4 5						
12	Difficulty						
13	Great Little						
14	1 2 3 4 5						
15	Time						
16	Great Little						
17	1 2 3 4 5						
18	Return on Investment						
19	Little Great						
20	1 2 3 4 5						
21	Resource Requirements						
22	Great Little						
23	1 2 3 4 5						
24	Total	0	0	0	0	0	0
25							

after format changes

	A	B	C	D	E	F	G
1	**Problem Selection Matrix**						
2	*A decision aid for prioritizing issues*						
3							
4		Option	Option	Option	Option	Option	Option
5	Control	A	B	C	D	E	F
6	Little Great						
7	1 2 3 4 5						
8	Importance						
9	Little Great						
10	1 2 3 4 5						
11	Difficulty						
12	Great Little						
13	1 2 3 4 5						
14	Time						
15	Great Little						
16	1 2 3 4 5						
17	Return on Investment						
18	Little Great						
19	1 2 3 4 5						
20	Resource Requirements						
21	Great Little						
22	1 2 3 4 5						
23	Total	0	0	0	0	0	0
24							

This spreadsheet is atypical. It might be used for selecting an option at a meeting where an overhead projector is available. What do you think the shaded version does better? The intent was to give the eye a focus and make it clearer where to place the numbers.

Sometimes the data can say it all—or at least most of it—as in the Flowerz n Bulbz sales report. Cell borders are removed in both versions, but the clearer version shows quarterly and yearly totals shaded and enlarged to focus the reader's attention. It's clear that sales increased overall. But what about why? That's not clear. In the case of Flowerz n Bulbz, we might guess that purchases pick up in the planting months of spring, summer, and fall, and Christmas purchases give the fourth quarter a boost. But we don't know that.

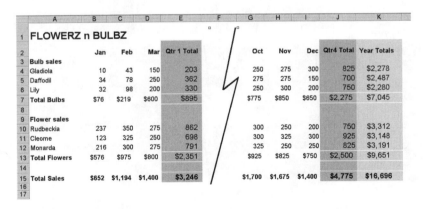

before format changes

after format changes

Annotating a spreadsheet is vital if the numbers cannot say it all. In the case of a budget, annotation is critical. Few of us can look at a budget and know the reason behind each number's value. I can't do that even when I've developed the budget myself. I need reminders about how I arrived at those numbers. If the text needs only to remind you or the user of how you derived the number, add a comment within the cell. In Excel, comments are flagged by a red triangle in the corner of the cell. Anyone with the digital version of the spreadsheet can read the comments by passing the mouse over the cells, but be sure not to hide critical information from recipients who will only have access to a paper version.

When the text you add to the spreadsheet must be immediately apparent to the reader in order to permit understanding of numeric entries, include a text box nearby or include footnotes at the bottom of the page, as in the nonprofit budget example below. Each entry that could be questioned is annotated clearly by budget code. Seems like a simple thing, but it is so rarely done at all. Often, when it is done, the description is kept on a page separate from the spreadsheet.

		Budget Qtr 1	Actual Qtr 1	Budget Qtr 4	Actual Qtr 4	YTD Budget	YTD Actual	over -under
	Non Profit Organization BUDGET CENTER 10-- administration							
	Budgeted and Actual Expenses for fiscal year 2001							
Line Item #	Revenue							
150	Interest	100	99	115	102	440	429	-11
200	Dividends	55	60	55	106	220	285	65
	Total Revenue	155	159	170	208	660	714	54
	Expenses							
100	Bulk Mail Allocations	300	270			300	270	-30
101	Copies	12	5	12	5	48	230	182
102	Food	60	50	60	71	240	230	-10
104	Postage	35	33	50	78	170	185	15
106	Supplies	50	40	50	40	200	206	6
201	Stationery	350	25			350	25	-325
204	Liability Insurance					250	250	0
208	Tax Return Prep.					230	260	30
209	Telephone	30	56	30	42	120	161	41
210	USPO Box Rental					65	44	-21
211	USPO Bulk Permit	100	100			100	100	0
	Total Expenses	937	579	202	236	2,073	1,961	-112

Notes
100 Bulk mail re-allocated to other expense areas based upon usage by program
101 Copies in Quarter 3 for newly developed operations manual
201 Stationery low but need to deplete old stock --purchase stock with new logo next year
208 Tax return prep fee increase due to added program areas --increase in next year's budget
209 Increase in out-of-town members this year --plan to use email more

The example shows budgeted and actual administrative spending for a nonprofit organization. Every other row is shaded to permit scanning across a budget code. Actual values have been formatted to display red if the amount expended is over the budgeted amount (this is done through "conditional formatting," where a value greater or less than another value causes the display to be formatted in a specific way). The red values are shown bold and gray here.

Quarters are set off from one another, also. The notes, listed in order of budget code, explain budget variances or serve as reminders for the preparation of the next year's budget. Since budgets are generally completed annually, giving the budget preparer all the information in one place certainly makes for a more efficient process.

Got gobs of data in a list? Save your readers the time and effort of reviewing an entire list of data. Spreadsheet software will permit you to hide the detail data and show only the subtotals and totals. An outline symbol at the left of the data shows that the list is summarized and, in the electronic version, may be opened to reveal detail.

Tips: There are simple techniques to making your spreadsheet much more inviting and readable—and fun to produce:

— Turn off the gridlines.

— Enlarge and bold the headings.

— Align most text left.

— Align text describing totals right.

— Adjust row width to cell entries.

— Format currency without decimals, if possible.

— Use color or gray to shade rows and columns that must stand out or that permit reading across a long row of cells.

— Use the drawing tools to circle a number, point at a total, display a text box.

INFORMATION DESIGN DESK REFERENCE

reports and manuals

Writing a report or a manual can seem daunting if you do it infrequently. There's so much to research and organize. Then you have to glue it all together with a narrative. How can it be done quickly and clearly?

speed the process

The fastest way to get a long document started and to edit it in progress is to use outline view. Using outline view requires that you use **styles** to identify different levels of headings and distinguish them from normal text. Once you have defined a hierarchy of headings (even two levels—heading and normal is fine for a report), you can reap the benefits. Type in your outline, or at least several headings as placeholders; you'll fill in the detail later. Be sure the text is actually defined as Heading 1, Heading 2, etc. (You can rename them—they don't have to be called Heading 1 and so on, but those are default names in MS Word.) Begin to fill in content as normal text.

Now, view the document in outline view. I just did that for this book. I'm currently filling in normal text in a section under a Heading 4-level subtitle. When I look at this document in outline view, I see a simple list of subtitles, indented according to their level. I can

---

```
OUTLINE VIEW
     1  2  3
Heading 1
   Subheading 1
      Text 1
Heading 2
   Subheading 2
      Text 2
Heading 3
   Subheading 3
      Text 3
```

```
OUTLINE VIEW
     1  2
Heading 1
   Subheading 1

Heading 2
   Subheading 2

Heading 3
   Subheading 3
```

OUTLINE VIEW
|
Heading 1
Heading 2
Heading 3

move entire sections around to change order in outline view; this makes it much easier to think through sequencing of large amounts of content. You will much prefer editing large segments in outline view to trying to scroll around through the document, cutting and pasting!

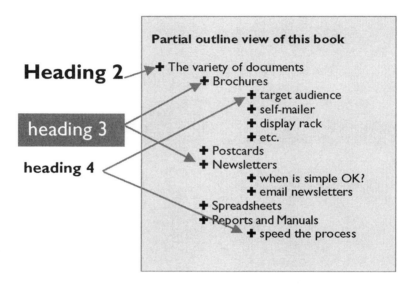

Heading 2

heading 3

heading 4

Partial outline view of this book

+ The variety of documents
  + Brochures
    + target audience
    + self-mailer
    + display rack
    + etc.
  + Postcards
  + Newsletters
    + when is simple OK?
    + email newsletters
  + Spreadsheets
  + Reports and Manuals
    + speed the process

The tools in outline view permit you to move content around and to "demote" text to a lower level (more indented) or "promote" it to a higher level, thereby refining the outline and your subheadings. If you were to place the cursor next to the plus by the word Brochures, in my outline, and you clicked on the minus sign in the tool bar, you would see all the Heading 4 items under Brochures disappear. In a similar way outline view lets you hide any of the detail levels globally by clicking on the number 1, 2, 3, etc. on the toolbar. Say I wanted to look at only Heading 2-level items for this entire book. I would click on the 2 on the tool bar in outline view and the screen would look like the box below. I had to do it, since I can't remember without looking.

Heading 2 level

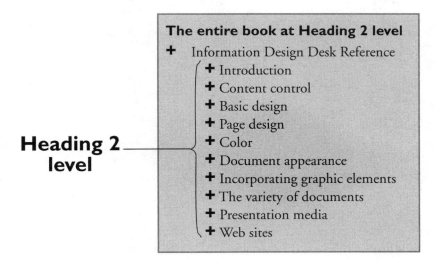

The entire book at Heading 2 level

+ Information Design Desk Reference
  + Introduction
  + Content control
  + Basic design
  + Page design
  + Color
  + Document appearance
  + Incorporating graphic elements
  + The variety of documents
  + Presentation media
  + Web sites

This is exactly what I did to decide how to sequence the major sections of this book. I originally had the document appearance section before the color section and then changed my mind. All I had to do was use the up arrow on the tool bar, or I could paint and drag the section I wanted to a new location. All supporting headings and content go with the higher-level headings in a move. This makes the big document much less daunting! Now you're ready to start your own version of *Ulysses* or *War and Peace*.

From outline to presentation. One more really great thing that creating an outline can do for you: you can insert a formatted outline into your presentation software and "poof" you have the beginnings of a presentation. Heading 1 becomes the title; Heading 2 becomes the first level of text, and so on.

Document map. If all you want to do is find different locations in your document easily, Word has a document map that allows you to see where you are in the document and to go to a different location at a click. It looks like the outline, but it sits at the side of your screen as you type with your document in normal or page view. It's so nice to see things in context.

> It's your turn to try it. Create a test document, insert some content (or open an existing document and save it with another name), and apply a style with at least two levels of headings. Look at it in outline view, move sections around, and then check it in normal view. Now have a look at the document map: what happens to your document view if you click on a heading in the document map list?

format

Check your word-processing application. Chances are you have some templates there that you will find very handy. Templates contain every format and style option right there for you to see. Once you find one you like, all you have to do is replace it with your content; the template establishes how numbered lists, bullets, tables, headings, and other components will look. I wish I'd done that before I started this book. But I often do things the hard way, so I created my own style for this book.

> As an exercise, go fire up that word-processing application and find a template you like. Add content from something you recently wrote or write something new. Pull in a chart or table from a spreadsheet. Add a graphic (maybe a logo you use). Look good?

Table of contents. Here's another benefit of using styles to format your document: you can create a table of contents automatically. That's very useful, particularly if your document is long or you are stringing a number of files together in a Master Document. Entries in tables of contents generated automatically in this way can be used as links to locations within your documents. So you can save your file as a regular document, as an Adobe Acrobat PDF, or as HTML, and your online reader can link to different areas in your document from the table of contents. Makes online reading more pleasant.

Since we're on the subject—do make your table of contents more valuable than a simple list of headings and page numbers. In this book I've provided two tables of contents to allow readers involved in a specific project a way to find all the related topics. Give readers an idea of the types of content and the relative significance of various content within the document. The following table of contents is from a manual I created for patients of a midwifery practice. What can you tell by looking at this table of contents?

— Section numbers indicate the beginning of a topic. Pages are numbered within the topic: Prenatal Exercises—Page 2, etc.

— The manual focuses on prenatal care, listing more detailed content. Don't be afraid to have the same kind of asymmetry in a table of contents. Since prenatal care is the focus, there is no reason to pad the section on childbirth with more supporting detail. This is intended for the expectant mother's use, and brevity—as much as reasonably possible—is important.

— It contains several participative sections to involve the expectant mother in her own care. Those interactive sections are shown in bold.

— Urgent issues are listed right up front, and the content is placed in the front pocket (the content consists of two posters the expectant mother can put inside a cupboard door along with multiple copies of a chart intended for daily use).

PREGNANCY, CHILDBIRTH AND POST-PARTUM CARE

a guide for clients of Marilee Wells, LM

PREGNANCY _____ SECTION

Urgent issues
    When to call me _____ front pocket
    Warning signs of pre-term labor _____ front pocket
    Kick counts* _____ front pocket

Getting ready for your baby
    Preparation diary* _____ 1
    Bill of Rights _____ 2
    Birth is not an illness! _____ 3
    Monthly signs and symptoms _____ 4

Healthful diet
    Dangers of a bad diet _____ 5
    Good foods help you and your baby to stay healthy _____ 6
    Food diary form* _____ 7
    Your guide to healthful eating* _____ 8
    Guide to vitamins and minerals _____ 9
    Do not eat or take... _____ 10

Self-care
    Remedies for discomforts _____ 11
    Prenatal exercises _____ 12

What to expect
    Your baby's development _____ 13
    Preparing for breast-feeding: flat or inverted nipples _____ 14
    Sex during pregnancy _____ 15
    Tests during pregnancy _____ 16

CHILDBIRTH _____ SECTION

Labor and delivery guide _____ 17

Labor—from start to finish _____ 18

Cervical dilation _____ 19

POST-PARTUM CARE _____ SECTION

Post-partum instructions _____ 20

Post-partum exercises _____ 21

Breastfeeding—getting started _____ 22

Baby care _____ 2

*Items in bold are interactive: you'll need a pen

An informative table of contents

version control

Handling revisions is difficult if you are working on a document with input from more than one other person. That's reality for those of us teaming up on projects. So here's a way to keep sane. Believe me, I've learned this the hard way. I am happy to spare you from learning from horrific mistakes, as I have.

Version numbers or dates of revision are a must. I once thought I'd be working with only one reviewer, and our plan was to email the several documents I was creating back and forth. I'm ashamed to admit it, but I thought the email date stamp could serve as my version control. Wrong. Suddenly, I began receiving revisions, unexpectedly, from other people, each working from a slightly different version of the different documents. I learned my lesson.

Put the date or version number in the footer or header. The document you see shows an automatically generated date in the header or footer. I can't believe I didn't bother to do this with that situation I described, because it's so easy.

Create a separate document listing only changes. One way to ensure that you get changes or recommendations in a format you can handle is to ask reviewers to send changes only by listing the section to replace and the text to be replaced. This takes much longer for the editor, so you'd use it for a critical document. For example:

"Under heading, Summary of Findings, replace text 'we looked at' with 'we observed.'"

A bright color for changes. I always ask reviewers of paper and online documents to make their changes in red. It's easy to change type colors electronically and, when I'm editing a document for a client, I like to use the other options, like strikethrough. Word processing applications can track changes automatically, too.

Let the software do it. Word processing applications can track changes for you—if the people you are working with are willing to use this feature.

forms

If you're like me, you can't stand filling out forms. That's why I'm including them here. They're often a pain to complete because they're poorly designed. If they're not easy to fill out, chances are they won't be filled out at all or, as in the case of the 2000 U.S. presidential election, they will be completed haphazardly. If you create a form, you probably have some hope that it will be completed. Perhaps you are creating a job application form or a customer-service survey. You want to be certain your forms can do their job.

One caution about forms before we start: I work in the training and development field. Nobody loves forms more than trainers and, frankly, a lot of forms we create are just plain nonsense. But the first thing to ask is, is it reasonable to ask that this information be entered into this separate form? Quite often we ask people to transfer information from one place to another, when a different (perhaps automated) solution might be more elegant. So this discussion of forms is not an endorsement of their indiscriminate use.

the basics

There are some basic things your form will need to contain.

Title: What is this form for? The title should answer this question for the USER, not for you. So if you give someone your job application form # JA102 to complete, that form number cannot serve as a title. It should say, "Application for Employment, Mercy Hospital." In small letters at the bottom corner you can reference form #JA102. Only the IRS gets away with asking everyone to reference forms by their numbers.

Directions: How do I fill this thing out? Do you want me to circle my answer or fill in a box? Are the areas for answers lined up directly with the questions, or are answers placed in separate locations? People are not eager to read directions anyway, so unavoidable questions and their related directions need to be close together. If the special instructions for item 8 are next to item 8, you have a better chance of getting people to comply.

Test your form on some representatives of the user group, and check their surprising responses to the directions. That'll help you clarify those directions! Do tell the person where to send or take the form when it's complete, too.

Data fields: What do I put in this space? Do I write above or below the line? Be clear about what you want. If the form says "date," does that mean today's date? Be sure all the fields mean something to your target group. We've all tried to complete forms with utterly incomprehensible fields. What does EIN mean to most people? It means Employer Identification Number to me, but what if I'm interpreting that wrong, and it really means something else?

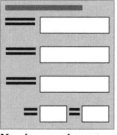

You know where to write on this form.

Another way to clarify data fields is to shade the areas where you don't want people to write, as in the example at left. This works better than a warning not to make any stray marks outside the lines.

More questions to consider about data:

— Are the data from the form going to be **entered manually** into an existing database? Then have some pity on the data-entry people, and set up the data fields on the form in the order of their data-entry screens.

— Do numeric entries into the data fields need to be **summed?** Think of an order form or a tax form (sorry). The fields to be added together must line up. Areas where subtotals are calculated should be clearly set off from the areas where combined totals are entered.

— **How long** do the data fields need to be? Allow too much space for a short item, and people will spend time second-guessing their short answers.

— Do some **data fields rely on the content of other** data fields? For example, "Have you ever been convicted of a felony?" If the answer is yes, your respondent has to answer all the related questions probing the ugly details. Those with a clean record are directed to the next question.

PATIENT REGISTRATION FORM

PRF-1
10/97

Please complete the information below and return to the receptionist.

PATIENT'S NAME			DOB / /
SEX	SS# / /	MARITAL STATUS	MAIDEN NAME
MOTHER'S NAME			FATHER'S NAME
PATIENT'S ADDRESS			APT #
CITY	STATE		ZIP CODE
HOME PHONE		PRIMARY CARE PROVIDER	

PATIENT'S EMPLOYER		OCCUPATION	
ADDRESS			
CITY		STATE	ZIP CODE
EMPLOYMENT STATUS		WORK PHONE	EXT
NEXT OF KIN			RELATIONSHIP
HOME PHONE		WORK PHONE	EXT
CHIEF COMPLAINT			DATE OF ONSET

GUARANTOR'S NAME			RELATIONSHIP
DOB / /		SEX	SS #
ADDRESS			APT #
CITY		STATE	ZIP CODE
HOME PHONE		WORK PHONE	EXT
EMPLOYER		OCCUPATION	EMPLOYMENT STATUS
INSURANCE CO.	CO #	PLAN #	POLICY #

Patient signature_____

Today's date_____

patient registration form—before

Patient Registration Form

Please complete the information below. Circle selections where required.

Patient

Date of birth ___ / ___ / ___   Sex M F
MM / DD / YYYY   circle one

Marital status Single Married Separated Divorced
circle one

Maiden name _____

Social Security # _____-____-_____

Name _____

Address _____ Apt ____

City _____ State ____

Zip _____-____ Home phone ____-____-_____

Primary care physician _____

Patient's family

Mother's name _____
(unique identifier)

Father's name _____
(unique identifier)

Next of kin _____
(emergency contact)

Relationship _____

Home phone _____-____-____

Work phone _____-____-____ ext.____

Patient's employment

Occupation _____

Employment status Full Time Part Time Not Employed Retired
circle one

Employer _____

Employer address _____

City _____ State ____

Zip _____-____ Work phone ____-____-____ ext.____

Patient visit

Reason for visit _____   Date of onset ___ / ___ / ___
MM / DD / YYYY

Policyholder

Policyholder's name _____

Address _____

City _____ State ____

Zip _____-____

Home phone _____-____-____

Policyholder's relationship to patient _____

Occupation _____

Employment status Full Time Part Time Not Employed Retired
circle one

Employer _____

Work phone ____-____-____ ext.____

Insurance

Insurance co _____   Company # _____ Plan # _____ Policy # _____

Patient signature _____

Today's date _____

Please return completed form to receptionist.

Revision 10/1997   Form Number PRF-1

patient registration form—after

The registration form is shown here before and after some significant editing. This is a document that can make the difference between producing an accurate bill and producing a write-off. The format of the "before version" is daunting to both the person completing it and to the person with the task of entering the content into the patient database. The "before" version is very undifferentiated and could be unclear on many levels:

— Lines for data-entry categories merge into one another. How much space is really allocated to City, State, Zip Code?

— Completion of some of the fields requires additional explanation. Most of us would wonder how to complete the employment status field, for example. The revision includes a set of answers from which to select.

— Some categories of information are puzzling. Many people wanted to know why the heck we were asking for mother's and father's names or for names of next of kin. There were solid reasons. Without a unique identifier like Mother's name, all the Mary Smiths in the database might become a bit difficult to distinguish from one another. A serious medical error could result if information from one Mary Smith went into the other Mary Smith's file.

— Language is used in the unrevised form that might be a show-stopper. What is a "provider?" Better to say physician, since an MD is needed for the patient's record. What is a "guarantor?" This is the person who guarantees that the fee will be paid because he holds the policy for the patient's insurance. Well, how about calling "guarantor" a "policyholder"?

— Fields are listed from left to right in the exact order in which they appear in the database entry form. Despite that arrangement, the format doesn't lend itself to easy scanning by the data-entry person. It would be hard to take your eyes off the page and get back to the spot where you left off. In the revision, information is left in groupings that seem to belong together, while their proximity for data entry purposes is retained. For example: name, address, city, state, and zip are grouped into one area, with a left margin discernible by alignment of elements and use of bold type. Use of shading and labeling of data category (family, employment) also aid a successful data entry effort. Probably my only claim to fame at the Medical Center was with the data-entry group. They constantly reminded me that I was the ONLY person who had ever come to them for input BEFORE a form was designed. Needless to say, I was popular in that office. If you learn anything from this chapter on forms, I hope it is this: the people who need to transfer information from any form you devise should have a role in designing that form, just as the users should evaluate it for clarity and ease of use once it is in pilot phase.

A final checklist, then, for devising a form would be as follows:

1   Is it really **needed,** or is there a better way to capture this information?

2   Have you enlisted the **guidance** of the people who will need to use the form to do their work?

3   Have you conducted a **pilot** evaluation to determine if the form elicits the responses you expected?

online forms

If you have a population with access to computers to complete your form, you can reap the real benefits of placing your form online. Most benefits aid data integrity.

Space is not a problem.   It's easy to place directions next to each question, since you have plenty of space or access to optional features where directions can appear on "mouseover," and such.

Menus of answers limit errors.   Each question can have a pull-down menu of responses to ensure that the respondent selects from an array of valid answer to your question.

Programming can flag invalid entries. Even if fill-in fields are used, it is possible to place a series of suggestions next to the field or program edits that will flag invalid or nonexistent entries.

Programming can force the selection of only one choice.   Items with only one valid answer can be programmed to toggle between choices, making it impossible to check more than one answer.

| Frequently |
| Occasionally |
| Rarely |
| Not applicable |

Pull-down selections from an online form: in this case, the respondent is selecting the grayed word, which will appear in the window above.

⊙ ○
Yes No

A toggle field will allow only one selection to be made.

Mandatory fields can be created. Mandatory fields, if left incomplete, make it impossible for the respondent to move on without an entry.

Help is available. Respondents can ask for help with puzzling questions by clicking on a question mark or by placing a question mark within the field.

Tabulation can be programmed. You don't have to slog through piles of forms—the data are there in one location and can be ported into a statistical application or spreadsheet.

the survey: a special form of form

One type of form we see frequently is the survey. Everyone is doing follow-up customer service surveys—well, everyone with decent customer service seems to be doing them. Those with crummy customer service seem to prefer not to know what we think. Anyway, creating a survey for research purposes takes some special skill. But, many of us simply need to assess some needs or find out some opinions, and surveys are very useful devices.

Surveys require a careful pilot, since you can't be there to explain the questions once they're distributed. The questionnaire's instructions and questions must be perfectly clear! There are many ways to structure questions, based on the kind of data you need to collect. If you want qualitative data, you can ask open-ended questions. If you need to quantify the results, your questions should have a finite set of choices.

Genesee Survey Services of Rochester, New York provides custom employee surveys for organizations. They have a breadth of experience in creating survey questions and have kindly allowed me to include some of their excellent guidelines for writing questions here. Their examples are from employee surveying, but the examples bring the guidelines to life.

Genesee Survey Services: survey question guidelines

Keep it simple. Try to use single-syllable words, short sentences, and common language of the population that is to respond, e.g. "I like the kind of work I do." Avoid slang.

Avoid "double-barreled" items. When two questions are asked in the same sentence, there may be a positive feeling about one part and a negative feeling about the other. The word "and" is a good indicator of this type of question. If both items are necessary, use two separate questions.

Keep questions confined to issues people would know about. In general, it is best to ask individual opinions, e.g. "How satisfied are you with your opportunity to get a better job?" rather than "There is adequate opportunity for promotion."

Be as specific as possible. If you ask about each benefit specifically rather than seek a general assessment of benefits, you will get a different understanding. Some benefits may be assessed more highly than others. Also, make who or what you are referring to as clear as possible. If you are referring to supervisors, state that.

Use active voice. This will also help you to identify clearly to who or to what you are referring. Instead of "Sufficient effort is made to get the opinions of people who work here," write "My supervisor tries to get the opinions of people who work here." The verb "is" in the sentence is an indicator of passive voice.

Use references that are clear and use them consistently. Common phrases that work will are:

- The people I work with
- My work group
- My supervisor
- My supervisor's manager

Avoid negatively worded items. They are often confusing to those taking the survey and to those interpreting the results, since a negative response indicates a favorable situation.

Avoid extremes. It is not a good idea to use the words "always" or "never" in an item. A better way is using "almost always" or "almost never" both in the questions and in the response scale.

Write items that people care about. Those taking the survey will be more apt to respond if the content of the questionnaire reflects things they think are important, such as pay, benefits, opportunities, supervisory and peer relationships, security, work load, and so on.

Guidelines for scales. Pay as much attention to the scale as you do writing the item. Four scales tend to be the most useful and versatile:

Strongly agree. Agree. Neither agree nor disagree. Disagree. Strongly disagree.

Very satisfied. Satisfied. Neither satisfied nor dissatisfied. Dissatisfied. Very dissatisfied.

Very good. Good. Fair. Poor. Very poor.

Almost always. Usually. Sometimes. Not very often. Almost never.

Other scales can be used for special situations:
Far too much. Too much. About the amount. Too little. Far too little. (The middle response is favorable and the extremes are unfavorable.)

One of the best. Above average. About the same. Below average. One of the worst. (Good for comparisons.)

Much higher. Somewhat higher. About the same. Somewhat lower. Much lower. (Good for comparisons.)

Extremely important. Very important. Somewhat important. Not too important. Not at all important.

— Genesee Survey Services

What should a clear survey look like? You see a sample of what is known as a "smile sheet" entitled "Course Evaluation Survey." It's a fairly clear example. The topic statements lead into each item, decreasing the overall amount of reading required. These forms are handed out at the end of a program, when people are ready to bolt for the door. If you make it easy and fast to complete, they'll do it.

Name of course _____

Date(s) _____

COURSE EVALUATION SURVEY
Circle one number for each question.

	strongly disagree	disagree	neither agree nor disagree	agree	strongly agree
Program content					
— met stated objectives	1	2	3	4	5
— practical	1	2	3	4	5
— at an appropriate level of difficulty	1	2	3	4	5
— relevant to my job	1	2	3	4	5
— was satisfactory, overall	1	2	3	4	5
Program materials					
— consistent with the course objectives	1	2	3	4	5
— high quality	1	2	3	4	5
— easy to use	1	2	3	4	5
Instructor/facilitator					
— well prepared	1	2	3	4	5
— encouraged active class participation	1	2	3	4	5
— outstanding presentation skills	1	2	3	4	5
— handled questions effectively	1	2	3	4	5
Expectations for transfer					
— transferable to my job	1	2	3	4	5
— my supervisor will encourage me to use knowledge acquired here	1	2	3	4	5
— there are on-the-job barriers which will inhibit my use of the knowledge acquired here	1	2	3	4	5
— I plan to share what I have learned with my colleagues	1	2	3	4	5

General reaction, issues and recommendations (feel free to attach another sheet)

What were the most helpful parts of the program?

What were the least helpful parts of the program?

Describe barriers you anticipate in implementing what you have learned.

Please make additional comments for improving the training program.

Please return this survey to the address on the back of this form.

making it easy to tabulate

Looking at the Course Evaluation Survey you are probably thinking, "She violated her own rules—how would the data-entry person know what line the results belong with? There are no numbers for items!" Well, if this form were going to be keyed into a database by a data entry person or placed on a scanner, yes, I'd have to change it a bit and add item numbers. But these forms are often hand tabulated. To make it easy, I would create a template with the categories set up just as they are in the survey, with columns at the right. You might need more than one template sheet if you have many respondents. To make it simple, let's pretend that there are four respondents, and we will only show the program content section of results.

Program content	Joe	Sue	Bob	Pat
—— objectives	3	2	3	
—— practical	4	4	5	
—— difficulty	5	3	4	
—— relevant	5	5	5	
—— overall	4	3	4	

**Format for collecting data
manually from evaluation survey**

I added names to make it clear that the columns represent respondents. (The evaluation is not signed, so the forms could be numbered or labeled prior to tabulation.) **I would place each evaluation form over this template and line it up with the next empty column to the right.** Pat's scores are not entered yet, so I'd cover up the scores of Joe, Sue, and Bob and align the rows. The gray rule lines match the survey's lines, helping with alignment. It's a kluge, I admit. But many of us have no scanning equipment at our disposal.

If surveying is a big interest, or if you are getting serious about surveying, there's a great book by Earl Babbie, *Survey Research Methods,* you should have in your library. It's listed among the references here.

posters

Posters need to capture the attention of a moving audience. Since posters are viewed from a distance, one clear message, above all, needs enough emphasis to attract that attention. Good design, with visuals in harmonious relationship with text, should hold that audience's attention. Posters offer artistic freedom. There's no need for a grid, so you can create the composition you love.

Say Professor Rhyz is giving a talk next Thursday at the school of culinary arts. You'll email everyone you can, but you really want to reach a larger audience. Those hallways will look better adorned with one of your poster creations. How do you get their attention? First, be sure you start with letters that can be read from the expected distance. Letters two inches high may be readable up to 20 feet, but the typeface will affect legibility. Test! If your poster is primarily text, you'll need to draw readers in with a few large words.

The audience for posters is random, so you need to make it noticeable. What is most important about the professor's talk? If it is the subject, bread baking in this case, a related graphic with the topic in large type should get attention. Or, is it most significant that he was honored by the famous Remulak Culinary Association, which brought him great notoriety in the field? Then, you might have his picture on the poster if he's interesting-looking or well known. Key information should be the prominent feature of the poster.

Look at some posters at the local frame shop. Decide which ones work for you. Then start sketching some ideas. As in every other printed item, restraint often has a greater impact than abundance. Keep it simple, and you will attract more viewers. A poster can't pack in every detail; that's not its purpose. Give viewers a phone number or Web site for more information.

Look at lists of words that get attention. Advertisers use them all the time—words like *new or you*. Once you have viewers' attention, keep it by offering a benefit. Why would I want to hear Professor Rhyz expound on yeastless breads? He is an expert in air leavening. So, the benefit to bread bakers is that there is still a way to make bread when they've run out of yeast. Headline? "Out of yeast?" That might stop the random baker from walking by and pull him in to find out why you're asking. Then give him the facts. If you are using an illustration, make sure it is in harmony with the key information in the copy. I used a hand holding a jar of yeast almost upside down—it's eye-catching because its diagonal line depicts a bit of movement. You might have to use a photograph and scan it (if you don't use a digital camera). I modified the photo in the poster shown here with a quick filter effect in a photo-editing application—the only time I used anything other than standard word-processing, presentation, or spreadsheet software in this entire book—to make it look more like a drawing than a photo.

What do you do when you're

out of yeast ?

use **air leavening!**
Professor Rhyz will be here to
demonstrate this simple process.

Rhyz, Remulak Culinary Association
honoree, is the leading authority on
the chemistry of bread baking.
Students and local bakers welcome!

June 29, 2001
2:00 PM
Bakery Auditorium

Posters can be free form, but you will need to plan the layout before
executing it. Posters get more attention if there is some action within
them. Depending on colors and composition, if all the lines are horizontal or vertical, it will look somewhat static. Action can be
achieved simply with some diagonals. In the following example, the
unseen lines lead the reader's eyes from the boats, to the title, to the
supporting information.

Be sure to provide just the minimum information. Keep the word count low so that your illustration or main point can stand out.

TOY BOAT REGATTA!
————Shelter Cove, June 28————

Enter your homemade craft by **June 1**
and raise money for **Easter Seals!**

craft guidelines & sponsorship rules
www.toyboatregatta.org
716.555.4321

You'll need two copies of a poster. Analyze the poster's design. Then, redesign it by cutting it up and repositioning elements. Try to maintain a clear hierarchy of information, but in a new arrangement. Were you able to improve the impact?

Think of a movie you liked. Then decide on a theme for a poster. Type a few descriptive words or phrases to describe it, using a typeface that fits the mood of the film. Then, sketch (or cut from a magazine) visuals that match the words. Arrange them in different layouts and analyze why the layouts work or do not work.

wall charts

Most workplaces need some reminders around of progress on a project or a description of a critical procedure, such as proper pre-
surgery hand-washing technique. While posters can be arranged
quite freely, it is best to start with a grid for a wall chart. Wall charts
should be attractive but, the elements should be arranged in an orderly fashion.

You generally know the audience for a wall chart, and you aren't trying to "Wow!" them, only to inform them. The materials should
match the use: if you are tracking monthly sales or defects per unit,
the chart is a living document. Rather than expect all the people involved to write the updates on the chart neatly, provide them with
magnets or tacks that they can insert into the intersection of the axes
on the chart. If the wall chart conveys a procedure, do it with pictures whenever possible. Pictures are absorbed much more quickly
than words and they are retained.

The wall chart here is text-only, because the audience, people learning about performance management, is interested in the content.
Further use of graphics could distract readers from the flow of the
chart. The chart requires the ability to follow the thread of the

thought. But it is a handy tool. What do you do if a person couldn't do a new task if you put a gun to his head (as Robert Mager would say)? Look at the chart and find the answer. Yes, it's a skill deficiency. No, he hasn't done it previously, so hold your fire. Some training is in order. Or what if he knows how to use the new engineering design system, but none of the needed tools are available? Get rid of the obstacle and get those tools.

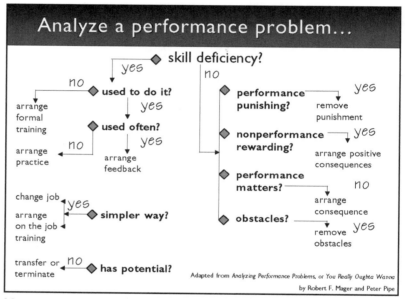

Analyze a performance problem...

Adapted from *Analyzing Performance Problems, or You Really Oughta Wanna* by Robert F. Mager and Peter Pipe

I know some managers who like referring to this chart.

Do you have a project underway? Create a wall chart with milestones and dates that participants can mark to indicate on-time completions and missed dates.

job aids

Folks call them "cheat sheets" and performance technologists call them performance-support tools. Whatever you call them, they are tools to help people do their jobs and increase the quality of their performance. The quick-reference flow chart for routing a prescription request, on page 159, is an example of a job aid. Job aids provide help with completing a task at the time the task needs to be done.

Most of us have created a job aid for our own use. We've listed the steps for a procedure that we don't follow often enough to commit to memory, such as programming a VCR or creating a chart in a spreadsheet program. But if you are a manager, or someone responsible for accuracy, you know that "cheat sheets" created on the fly can sometimes be inaccurate. I remember checking the "cheat sheets" used by the billing staff in the ambulatory care clinics of the medical center where I worked. Each person had written down the most frequently used visit and ICD-9 codes, to avoid taking the time to do a look-up in the large books. Not surprisingly, billing wasn't very accurate. In order to improve the financial performance of the clinics, I had Medical Records verify the "cheat sheets." With the help of Medical Records, I pulled together one accurate cheat sheet for each clinical area, with a plan to review and update it annually.

establish the need

How do you know if you need a job aid? Ask yourself the following questions:

— **Is the task completed infrequently?** In the example, the billers listed the most frequently used codes.

— **Is it complex, or does it require precision?** In the biller example, precision is key. If they choose an incorrect code, billing is inaccurate and no payment results. Job aids, in this case, had a direct payoff.

— **Are changes frequent?** Billing codes change each year. Last year's "cheat sheet" will produce errors in this year's bills.

— **Are errors costly?** Yes, in the billing example, very costly. Every inaccurate billing code caused a bill to be rejected (read: NOT paid) by insurance companies.

types of job aids

What does a job aid look like?

A job aid can take the form of a checklist, a procedure, a matrix, a worksheet, a decision table, a flow chart, or any combination of these. The most important thing to remember is that job aids provide only the most critical, specific information, as simply as possible. A job aid gives a clear picture of the end state or outcome. The user must know when she is "done."

Which type of job aid is used for which performance?

The list below describes job aids, and their applications, in order of increasing complexity.

Job aid	Defined	Example
check list ✔ Do this ✔ Do something else ✔ Look at that ✔ Read that	A list of tasks that do not need to be performed in any specific order.	List of items to assemble before completing income taxes.
procedure Step / What to do 1 Find the leash. 2 Find the dog. 3 Hook leash to dog collar. 4 Commence walking.	A list of tasks performed in a specific order.	Step-by-step calculations to determine taxable income.
matrix Dogs / Small / Medium / Large Friendly Dachshund Springer Labrador Protective Schnauzer Shepherd Doberman Mellow Westie Bull dog Bernese	Two or more lists intersecting to form a table, such as this.	Quick look-up table—to determine tax amount, or to find the right billing code.
work sheet worksheet	A form with blanks to complete with calculations or information.	Income tax form, order form.

decision table/ decision tree 	Table/matrix is used to select from alternatives, potential conditions or outcomes. Decision tree is graphic and can convey a hierarchy of independent conditions and the outcome resulting from their combinations.	Determine insurance premium entry requirements for a program.
flow chart 	A set of predetermined procedures to achieve an outcome.	- Determine entry requirements for a tournament. - Flow chart for a prescription request on page 159.

To reap the benefits, job aids need to appear in a place where they are integral to the work. They have the potential to reduce inefficiency and boost motivation by helping people to feel more secure about their work.

> Think of an example of a task you perform infrequently enough to make it necessary to pull out the documentation, but not frequently enough to keep that documentation handy on top of your desk. One example might be directions for making a conference call. Create a flow chart style job aid with the key directions that will cue you immediately. Perhaps you can hide it under the phone.

résumés

Your résumé is your marketing stratagem. Not that you should make it especially creative! But if it doesn't command attention, get the message across clearly, and look polished, it won't be considered. As the cliché goes, you have seconds to make that impression, and if you don't, the cost could be significant. Actually, many organizations use machines to read résumés at the first pass. But humans see them next, and the overall impression needs to be of high quality.

There is good advice out there on content for your résumé. You have to pick what works for you. I've never been a fan of the "statement of objectives;" I've rarely seen one on a résumé that looked sincere or made much difference to my hiring decision. Written well, they can tell your reader what it is you want to do, but in my opinion, the cover letter is the best vehicle for this (with the exception of résumés posted on the Web, which are generally stand-alone; in which case definitely include that objective). If you plan to include an objective statement, have someone who looks at a lot of résumés read it to see if it conveys the message you intend. Don't make the mistake of simply changing the objective statement for different job applications; you'll probably need to edit the entire document for different positions. However, the safest advice, in the end, is to include a statement of objective for people who find it useful. People like me can ignore it.

basics for résumé content

Compile laundry lists. If you have lots of jobs in your work history, consider compiling them into rather abbreviated capability summaries and accomplishment lists. A great many jobs and titles could tend to confuse a recruiter, especially if they are not strictly related to one another. And any list should contain fewer than about six items. If you must include a long list, break it up by subject with subheadings.

Reduce words. Phrases like "I was responsible for…" and "duties included…" can be converted to bullets.

Use key words from the employer's ad or other information that describes your skills and experience—as long as they describe you accurately. If your résumé is going to a large organization or to a hiring agency, the chances are it will be scanned for key words to be sure it's a "fit" with the requirements of the job. You don't want to risk getting cut before a human lays eyes on your résumé. Key words are usually nouns that describe skills, jobs or education or technical terminology. Key words can include job titles you've held, educational degrees or certificates, skills, and any specific terms used in your particular field. The more key words, the more likely you are to get a "hit."

Use action language. Verbs like "reduced" or "spearheaded" or "created" convey more information than a phrase like "responsible for." Verbs are important to the human reviewer of your résumé.

Keep the focus on abilities and accomplishments. Tell reviewers about past performance that will lead to future success.

Photos or graphics? For most jobs you won't want to include a picture on your résumé. There are probably a number of situations where a photograph would be helpful—perhaps a sales position. I'd like to know that a salesperson I might hire had the ability to look approachable. But it's safest to omit the photograph if there is no particular need for it. Photos are used frequently on corporate biographies, however. And you frequently see them on Web résumés, to keep the content from seeming too remote and cold. If you are sending your résumé to an unknown location, or if you are pretty certain it will be scanned, DO NOT include any photo or graphic, or you will confuse the scanning device and make your creation look terrible.

résumé format

The usual design guidelines obtain:

Have some white space. People will want to write on your résumé. Make it easy for them. Plus, a dense gray page will look daunting.

Don't go line and box crazy. First, it often looks amateurish. More practically, if the résumé is to be scanned or copied, it will not reproduce well.

Use one style of type. If you're good, use two kinds of type—one for headings and one for body text. Because scanners and copiers might have a better look at your résumé than humans, you should use a standard typeface (no novelty type) and a font size of 10 or 12 points.

Use white paper. This one is hard for me to recommend, since I really enjoy a handsome stationery. But, the sad fact is your résumé will likely be photocopied or scanned more than once, so don't waste money on special colored paper. Regular-sized white or off-white will work best under most circumstances. Save the exciting colors for the résumé you post on your Web site.

Avoid excessive underlining, boldface, and italics. Even bullet points can be overdone.

chronological or functional?

This is said to be the big question, but you really need to provide a combination of the two. With the chronological format you show your experience in order, by position. A functional format allows you to present your skills primarily. You can't leave out a chronological work history, and you need to describe your skills separately, too. The real decision is around which category to emphasize.

Emphasize a chronological format if:

— you have a work history showing a progression to your current goal

— your work history is without significant gaps

— you are currently employed in the field

Emphasize a functional format if:

— you are seeking work in a different field

— you have a work history with significant gaps

— you have had numerous short-term jobs

— you are not employed

Then combine the best of both. With either main format, you should always provide a qualifications summary. If your work history is long, consider focusing on the skills, education, and accomplishments relevant to the position you seek and include only more recent positions, with a summary of work prior to fifteen years ago. If a full account of your employment history is needed, provide it in a separate section to permit quick review of the current information.

Before-and-after résumés illustrate some of these ideas. This young dog has limited experience, so she has listed hobbies and skills in case the reader is not sufficiently impressed with the jobs she has held. The picture is provided in the "after" version for fun, since she prefers the entrepreneurial atmosphere. If she were applying for a high-level corporate position, I'd advise her to get rid of the picture.

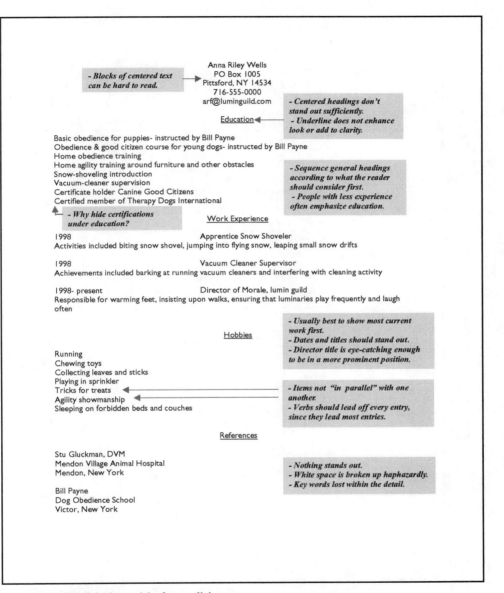

Anna Riley Wells' résumé before editing

Anna Riley Wells
PO Box 1005
Pittsford, NY 14534
716-555-0000
arf@luminguild.com

Work Experience

1998 - present   **Director of Morale**, *lumin guild*
Recognized with lofty title and plenty of biscuits. I warm feet, insist upon walks, ensure that
luminaries play frequently and laugh often.

1998   **Vacuum-cleaner supervisor**, *lumin guild*
Championship barking at running vacuum cleaners and interfering with cleaning activity led to
promotion within three months.

1998   **Apprentice snow-shoveler**, *lumin guild*
Master of biting snow shovels, jumping into flying snow, leaping small snowdrifts. I still perform
this duty seasonally, as requested.

Education

Basic obedience for puppies, instructed by Bill Payne
Obedience & good citizen course for young dogs, instructed by Bill Payne
Home obedience training
Home agility training around furniture and other obstacles
Snow shoveling introduction
Vacuum cleaner supervision

Certificates

Canine Good Citizen certificate
Therapy Dogs International member and certificate holder

Hobbies / Skills

Running
Chewing toys
Collecting leaves and sticks
Playing in sprinkler
Performing tricks for treats
Demonstrating agility showmanship
Sleeping on forbidden beds and couches

References

Stu Gluckman, DVM
Mendon Village Animal Hospital in Mendon, New York

Bill Payne
Dog Obedience School in Victor, New York

Anna Riley Wells' résumé after editing

emailing your résumé

Computer viruses have made attachments suspect. If you email a highly formatted résumé, your recipient might end up with lots of silly, useless characters, rendering your document very difficult to read. If you can't stand the thought of plain text and must offer your résumé electronically, you should post it as an HTML file on the Web.

I've mentioned some of the problems you can encounter if you add graphics to a résumé you plan to email. What can you do to make sure your résumé is readable and gets a hit? You're probably going to have to paste it into the body of an email message, so start by producing a file that can be read by any email application.

Font: When you look at your résumé in a plain text editor, like Notepad, you will see it in Courier or Monaco. Might as well start with one of these fonts; they do not permit proportional spacing. (And do check for surprises in a text editor.)

Text format: Keep the formatting down to plain text. Forget about bold, italics, and underline. Even tabs can get messy! Use the space bar (icky, but true). Just as in the newsletter example, use the asterisk or hyphen to substitute for actual bullets.

Page format: Not only can you not use the tab to indent, but you can't even set up more than one left margin, so headings have to be placed on a separate line.

Test: Save it as a text file, then send it to a buddy on a different platform (Mac or PC) and also send it to someone using a different application for email.

Presentation Media

Good visuals are mental shorthand.
Claire Raines and Linda Williamson

presentation media overview

One of the things I do in my work is define competencies for different organizations. Among the most frequently mentioned skills organizations require is the ability to convey a message clearly in a presentation. At some point in our working lives, we all need to create and deliver presentations.

We must consider many more factors in a live presentation of information than we do in a printed document because the media and the human deliverer have a great effect on delivery and audience response. The human connection is the far more important aspect of any live presentation, and an intimate group of three or four should receive more personal attention than an auditorium audience of two hundred. Think about your presentation as a people-to-people endeavor and your presentation media as the supporting cast.

Think back to presentations that impressed you. Usually the human interaction aspect of the presentation is the memorable part: the speaker's delivery and content are critical components. Ask, does this presentation need visual aids to be understood? Will visuals enhance the message? If they distract people from your message, they are harmful rather than helpful; visuals are compelling—they WILL command attention, good or bad. When the visuals were the memorable part, they generally have reached you on an emotional level.

The majority of the highest paid speakers use no visual aids at all. They have the good fortune to treat subjects they are passionate about. Plus, they know how to achieve rapport with the audience and get their points across through the force of their personalities. They would find a projector in their way—an unnecessary barrier. In fact, there are times when the equipment becomes the focus because of a problem. You spend the last half hour before your presentation fussing with the cords and connections when you could be talking with the early arrivals and finding out what they want to learn from your presentation. Establishing that rapport, when you are not already familiar with the audience, is far more important than the set-up of your projector.

Most of us are not earning five and six figure fees for one talk—we just need to deliver a cogent report to management. Visual aids are probably in order. However, remember the word "aid." The visuals you use should support your message; they cannot BE the message, unless you plan on being absent.

In preparing the sections on various media, I have recalled the teachings of a favorite professor, CJ Wallington, Ph.D. in the Instructional Technology program at Rochester Institute of Technology. I also included some of the tricks and hints I learned in a Robert F. Mager course on Instructor-Led Training, as well as my own experiences and biases.

establishing the need

How do you know your presentation will need visual aids? If you're an architect, it's much easier to show a picture of a building than to describe it! If you want funding for a decaying health center, a photograph will convey far more than words. But if all your visuals amount to an outline of your talk in bullet-point list form, think again. When have you enjoyed reading bullet lists from a projection screen? Do your audience a favor, and give them a condensed version of your talk on paper and keep the visuals to examples, pictures, charts or demonstrations that they will find enjoyable and more informative than text. Visual aids should reinforce your words, not merely repeat them.

plan ahead—the storyboard

If you decide you need to use some visuals, you'll still need to have a written document to work from—something that includes everything you want to say. Then you can create a storyboard to plan the sequence of your slides (either electronic or film) or overheads. If you put the storyboard together and adjust the sequence before committing to more formal design, you will save time and money on later editing, and your presentation will have a better flow.

A good storyboard looks like a set of thumbnail sketches of your presentation. A detailed storyboard is overkill for a small presentation but essential for organizing a large visual media presentation (overheads, slides, computer, video), particularly if you are outsourcing graphics, for example. One easy way to storyboard a short presentation, if you use a computer program like PowerPoint for slides or overheads, is to rough out ideas in a series of slides and sequence them in a slide sorter view.

A set of sample storyboard slides is shown on the following page. Note that it contains a title, a small amount of explanatory text, a graphic, and a place for version number and date. A storyboard really helps with sequencing and organizing a presentation.

confidentiality in health care

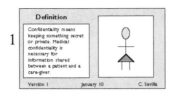
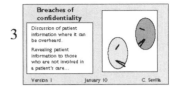

example storyboard

know the audience!

Facing an audience you know nothing about is terrifying. Do the research ahead of time. (See *analyzing a target audience* on page 7.) Talk to them as they come in the door. Find out why they came and where they're coming from. You'll be less nervous once you know more about them. Think about a speaker who seemed to know the audience well. You were impressed, most likely. I recently witnessed an amazing speaker, Dr. Marlene Caroselli, who arrived over an hour early, chatted with people as they came in, and just listened to the talk in the room prior to her presentation. She absorbed information about many of the people in the room and was able to focus on different people in the course of her talk, at times asking them questions she KNEW they could answer brilliantly. Did they love her? YES.

the handout

Most presenters provide a handout. It is expected. Think about what you would want to help you to retain the information. I've been asked, countless times, for a copy of my PowerPoint slides. It is hard to imagine anyone referencing them! I prefer to provide a summary outline of my talk. Properly formatted, a summary outline can be far more useful, easier to reference and less bulky to store. Besides, when I have worked hard on original graphics, I like to have sole use of them.

Presentation Handout
outline format
> summarize presentation
> <mark>highlight</mark> key points
> provide note space
graphics
> ensure graphics aid understanding
> minimize decorative graphics
> test a photocopy first, unless using printer
provide list of references, resources

A good summary should include all of the main points you will be making. You can use an agenda format if the presentation is part of a meeting. For a more formal presentation, make sure your outline follows your talk and highlight the items you want them to remember. Leave a margin on the side or between entries to allow note taking if you think it is likely that people will want to write notes. If there are any particularly explanatory graphics, include them. Include a reference list of the good resources you mention.

There are lots of ways to be innovative! Did you "mind-map" your talk? Give them a copy. Is your talk focused on a single model or program? Give them a diagram or chart that they can make their own notes on. It doesn't have to be an ordinary outline; if you want to make it zippy—do it!

The handout changes considerably if what you are doing becomes a training or teaching session. The principles are the same, but you will need to provide much more detail, along with exercises and practice for your learners. If this is new to you, work with an instructional designer to make sure your materials are sound.

check the venue/have a back-up plan

Another critical component of planning is to get a look at where you will be presenting, if possible. Always have a back-up plan. Have back-up overheads if the computer fails, have handouts you can speak from if there is no audio-visual equipment available. I created a PowerPoint work of art/masterpiece/wonderful presentation. OK, I thought so. I got started, and everything was fine and poof, the projector died. Well, lucky for me, some wiggling of chords got it working again, but I WAS prepared with handouts and extra exercises. Bring a power strip and extension cord along. Make sure you have it all with you by keeping a list of items you develop for the presentation as you develop them. I keep a list of each file I want to include in the handout, for example, and I use my generic checklist of items I need to bring with me.

Bring to presentation on Tuesday:
☐ Computer
☐ Mouse
☐ Power strip
☐ Extension cord
☐ Computer cors
☐ Projector
☐ Back-up diskettes of presentation
☐ Back-up overhead transparencies
☐ Copies of handout
☐ Lecture notes
☐ Pointer
☐ Business cards
☐ Brief bio for introduction

computer presentation checklist

practice, practice, practice

While I am not specifically talking information design here, the best designed presentation will not be effective without a presenter who can pull it off. Practice the presentation over and over. Give it to an audience of one dog or one truly good friend. Just saying it out loud will make you realize what needs editing. And going through the motions of using the equipment will help you realize where you need to stand and where things need to be placed. Besides, a friend will tell you where an illustration would be handy or where something was unclear. A dog will not be as instructive, so don't rely solely on the pooch.

the media decision

What is best to use: overheads, slides, computer presentation, or handout? There are other ways to go, such as flip charts, but they're more informal. You have the most flexibility with a handout and none of the complications of audiovisual equipment, but if you work with a handout alone, your presentation skills must be very good. If generating rapport and traveling in the audience during your talk are critical to your message, you might consider this lowest-tech approach. For formal and polished presentations, one of the three popular media works well. You need to know the advantages and disadvantages.

	Over heads	Slides	Computer presentation
Room bright?	✓		
Change order quickly?	✓		Only by stopping "show"
Notes on borders?	✓		
Minimal time to produce?	✓		
Use for medium-size (>25) audience?	✓	✓	✓
Use for large (>50) audience?	Depends on room	✓	✓
Emotional impact?		✓	✓
Include build effects?	✓	✓	✓
Speaker can see/monitor audience?	✓		
Speaker can face audience?	✓	✓	✓
Low cost to create?	✓		✓
Easy to modify for future presentations?	✓		✓
YOU ARE COMFORTABLE USING...			

INFORMATION DESIGN DESK REFERENCE

style guide for presentations

Be sure to set up a style guide for your presentations, too. There is a slide master in PowerPoint and in other presentation packages to make it easy to ensure that your slides have a unified look. The slide master dictates the position of elements on a screen, the size of the text, level of indentation, spacing, colors, and the background graphics. Many preset masters are available, so you can experiment with those on your way to creating your own master slides. If your presentation is long (either because you are spending a long time per slide or you have many slides), you will want to vary the look a bit, rather than simply following the master, to keep the audience interested. Use related colors and elements. You can check on your success by viewing your presentation in what is called "slide sorter view" in PowerPoint. If you've stayed within a palette of colors and a range of graphic styles, you will see a presentation that hangs together.

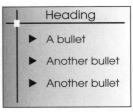

Sample text slide

Similarly, set up a style sheet for charts that you include in text documents. Always use consistent sizes of type for titles, labels, and so on throughout a document.

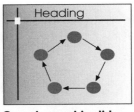

Sample graphic slide

Use a consistent style of artwork. Your document will be much more appealing if the artwork, clip art, or symbols look related to one another. These arrows all come from different "families" of arrows in Wingdings. Mix them in one document to direct your reader and you risk causing confusion. They won't look good together, either.

Choose one graphic style.

one last word

Whether you are delivering your presentation via electronic white board, Web conference, or flip chart, the same rules apply. It's about the people and the message. The supporting materials should not get in the way.

overheads

Overheads are the most popular presentation option. They're portable. Very little can go wrong. A bulb might burn out, but that's it. If you need to add a bit to your presentation, all you need is a printer or copier. The room can be somewhat more brightly lit than when a slide projector or computer projector is in use, so you can' see how your audience is reacting. The audience size can be very small to quite large. I've seen overheads used with an audience of more than two hundred, but that can be pushing it. If you're speaking to that many people and you have some time to prepare (it's not an ad hoc talk), a more polished presentation is in order. I used to be treated regularly to financial folks who took delight in showing an overhead slide of normal text size numbers (maybe 10 pt. Times Roman) on a spreadsheet as their contribution to a department-heads meeting in a large auditorium. Well, I guess we weren't supposed to see those numbers after all, were we?

44 pt. head

28 pt. text

Here are some hints for producing quality overhead transparencies:

Create a style sheet. Producing overheads is easiest with a presentation package like PowerPoint. There are built-in templates and master slides that you can use to keep everything consistent. For example, your titles should appear in a relatively consistent spot from transparency to transparency. The master slide allows you to set the size and style of type, heading or bullet locations, and sequence numbers for the entire presentation. You can set a template (many are available with the application) in the master slide to give your presentation a "look" of its own. Be careful not to choose a complex or dark background. I love dark, saturated colors, but they don't always project well; in fact, they can look dim and dingy. You want them to see what you've created, so stick to lighter colors until projection systems get more sophisticated.

Text. At minimum, use at least 40-point font size for headings or titles and 28 to 36 point for body text, as in the example. Seems large, but you shouldn't have gobs of text, only key words.

Lines of text. If you create an all-text transparency, keep the number of lines down to a maximum of six, if possible. Remember to incorporate some white space. Use only a few words per line to keep it from looking crowded. Of course, if you are describing a preexisting form or document, this doesn't apply. Simply make sure that members of your audience have exactly the same paper in their hands.

Builds. You can simulate a build effect with overlays of transparencies, kept in registration with one another. Don't use a colored background with overlays, or the result will be unreadable.

Landscape or portrait orientation. Overhead transparencies can be successfully oriented either way, but my favorite professor of instructional design convinced me that they tend to fit the image space of the projector a bit better when oriented horizontally. I am referring to the positioning of the standard 8.5-x-11 transparency on the lighted surface. Whatever you decide, first take a blank transparency and put it on the surface of the overhead. See how much is NOT going to project to your audience. With a felt-tip pen, mark up the edges of the area that will be projected. Measure the boundaries and make a template overhead to ensure that you do not exceed these boundaries.

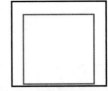

The projection area inside the lighted surface

Drawing with some precision. If you must create a drawing, or schematic, by hand, use graph paper, or an actual drawing, behind the transparency film. Or, use the drawing package in your presentation software.

Photographs. In general, photos don't do well when projected from an overhead. A good photograph showing the object of interest with no background distraction works best. If the subject is not isolated, the photograph will be difficult to "read." Also, high-contrast objects show up best on overheads. A subtly colored photograph will be hard to "read" also.

Frames. Test using frames (holders for the transparencies) for your presentation. They're a handy place to hide a few notes to yourself, and they keep the transparency films from sticking together. Mark the top center of a frame to make sure it is oriented correctly. Place a mark on the projector before you start, and you can line up all of your slides perfectly, without turning around to check on it. Keeps you facing forward!

Cartoons. Cartoons provide relief as nothing else can. But there are copyright laws, so be sure to check on permissions, or draw your own stick people.

Here are some hints for giving a quality presentation using an overhead projector:

Check ahead. Make sure the room really isn't too bright to permit seeing your transparencies. If you can darken the front of the room where you stand, your transparencies will look better.

Turn off the projector. When you are "between" overhead slides, and you plan to talk for a bit, the light and sound of the projector can be distracting. But don't go overboard. You don't need to turn off the projector every time you change to a new slide or talk for a minute; this can get terribly distracting.

Check for keystone effect. The farther the projector is placed from the screen, the greater the keystone effect. That's a characteristic of overhead projectors where the image looks larger at the top than at the bottom. (The effect gets its name from the keystone in an arch—it's the shape of the four-sided figure here.) See how far away you can be before keystoning distorts the image beyond acceptable limits. With larger audiences you want a large image projected on the screen, and if your screen is not tilted in at the top, keystoning will be a factor.

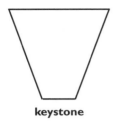

keystone

Organize before starting. Check the order before you start. That's simple. But don't (and I saw this done, too) take overhead slides out of a three-ring binder and place them back into the three-ring binder during the presentation. People are distracted by the neat-nik activity and lose focus on your talk. Also, unless you are a zealous three-ring devotee, try to use the transparencies outside of a binder holder. The extra transparency layers can make your image or writing look foggy, the last thing you want. Number them, either with a frame or a small piece of tape.

Progressive disclosure. This is where you reveal bullet points one by one. It's a style thing. If you give your audience a handout with your presentation content, the only reason to do progressive disclosure is to keep everyone focused on point (including you).

Position the projector where it will not obstruct the audience's view. Sounds obvious, but this is frequently a problem. Sometimes the room size does not permit placing the screen on the diagonal in one corner, and the projector in the other corner. The professor mentioned earlier, when presenting in a small room, always put the projector on a chair. The projector was never in anyone's way.

Writing on the transparency. This is a great way to capture audience input and record it for all to see, or demonstrate a concept. If your slides are black and white, you can add color to them with pens by circling important items for emphasis. That keeps your presentation engaging and draws attention exactly where you want it.

Look at the audience. Believe it or not, you'll be tempted to look at those overheads. If you can get someone to flip overheads onto the screen for you, you'll have a better chance. But if you need the notes you wrote on those frames, go ahead and do it yourself. Try to walk away from the projector a little bit and look at the people who came to hear you. If you are really glued to your notes, keep them separate from the slides in cards or a binder. You need to be able to move. Position yourself closer to the screen, where they will be looking, when you really want to deliver an important point.

slides

Slides still give an air of formality and polish. The big advantages slides offer compared to overheads include:

— Images are more **realistic** and can include full color.

— Photographs are **compelling** and beautiful.

— You can **switch slides remotely,** leaving you free to move around the room and relate easily to your audience.

— The **projector can be at the back** of the room (less distracting).

— The **light is even** (the light from most overhead projectors is bright in the middle, with a fall-off of light at the sides).

— Slides lend themselves to **stories.** You can build a story and gain a real emotional impact with a series of great photographs.

— You can use slides for the **largest of audiences,** up to several hundred people.

producing slides

Producing slides for a presentation can be simple: You can use your own camera for photographs, or you can purchase slides (check copyrights) for images you could never hope to capture.

If you do not have presentation software, there are services that will take your text information and create slides for you (see the description of text for overheads—the rules are the same). This is less expensive than it once was, but consider creating only what you know you will use over and over. Information that falls out of date quickly should be in a format that you can change easily.

Presentation software can create a set of slides very easily, through the use of a service bureau. Your slides will have a consistent, unified look and all you need to travel with is a set of slides, since most venues have a slide projector available. No need to bring your own computer and special projector.

giving an effective slide presentation:

Room lighting. Get there early enough to determine how dark the room will need to be for your slides to be visible. Thirty-five millimeter slides seem to look best when the background is dark, so you can't depend on the screen as a source of light. If the room must be very dark, be sure to interchange your use of slides in the talk with times when the room lights are on and you are engaging the group in discussion, for example. Dim lighting encourages snoozing after some time, and you need to monitor your audience before it's all over.

The slide tray. Keep your slides in a clean, dry place between presentations (dust is magnified when projected) and make sure that none are backwards or upside down. Nothing makes you look less credible than an occasional sideways image. Make sure the emulsion side of the slide "faces" toward the screen, away from the light source and that you have placed all images in the tray upside down. Once they're in the tray and you've previewed them, mark all the slides on one side of the top corner to ensure proper placement. Then, check the tray by viewing to avoid embarrassing surprises.

Builds and movement. You can create builds easily, to add bullet points, or to describe an object or concept. You can also sequence slides so that objects appear to move or change a bit (like time-lapse photography). If you're not a photo pro, slides made by a service bureau from your presentation software will achieve a simple build effect. However, if you really need full animation or movement, use a computer or a videotape.

presentation software

Computer applications offer easy access to a powerful multimedia presentation. Unfortunately, you have probably also seen some really disastrous results with a computer presentation. I witnessed a presentation to a group of about twenty-five people in 9-point font. The speaker said, "Hmm, I could see this on my computer but it doesn't show up on that screen." He ended up reading his presentation to us. Most presentations aren't that bad, but most I've seen aren't very good, either. Often they're text-only bores. Or, the graphics and colors are very, what's a polite word?…distracting. You can create a great presentation with just a little practice and some guidelines.

What is different about a computer presentation? I will list the significant advantages, then a few disadvantages. But first, there is one aspect that can be a positive or a negative. You can create a large number of many slides for your presentation—good if you are covering a complex topic over a long time, and bad if the presentation really should be short, and you are switching slides much more than three times per minute. You don't want your audience to get dizzy!

first the negatives

You have to haul heavy equipment. You'll need a laptop and a projection system. Occasionally, all the equipment is there for you and you need only bring your diskette. Most often, you'll haul.

Fear of equipment failure. With an overhead or slide projector a bulb can blow, but little else tends to fail. With computers, any number of things can go wrong. ALWAYS have a back-up plan. Have your presentation on a disk and carry a set of overheads of your presentation. At minimum, prepare to use the handout as a talking tool.

Learning the software. Fortunately, presentation applications are among the easiest to learn. However, if you want to include complex graphics, audio and video, there is a bit more learning to do.

What you see on the computer will look different on the screen. It's easy to be fooled into using a dark, dramatic background because it looks so good on your PC. You will need to check the presentation on a projection system to be sure that your colors look the way you intend them to look. On unsophisticated systems, saturated colors become very dark and difficult to distinguish. You're safest with light or white backgrounds and lighter, brighter colors. If you use a black background, bright colors and white elements will show up best. Use a light field with black type for longer passages of text, however.

Computer projectors are variable in light intensity and ability to reproduce what you have developed. If you are presenting to a very large audience (over one hundred people), the projector has to be of extremely high quality, or your images will appear washed out, fuzzy, or both.

more positives than negatives

Variety of speaker support aids. Your presentation file is easily converted to a handout, an outline, speaker notes, or even 35-

millimeter, or overhead slides (the latter are part of any back-up plan).

You can leave the computer at the office. If a computer, projector, and Web connection are available at the location of your talk, you can post the presentation to the Web. Freedom!

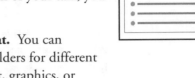

Slide layouts create consistency in graphic format. You can choose from a variety of layouts that create placeholders for different kinds of content, such as heading text, bulleted text, graphics, or charts. For example, the slide layout to the right shows a heading and bullet list.

The master slide keeps text formats and backgrounds consistent. Use the master slide to establish, for example, a whole presentation in bright blue Times Roman type, ranging from 44 to 32 point, with a light-gray gradient background and dark-gray border, as shown at right. You can change individual slides as the need arises, but you can always return to a consistent look.

If you create a color scheme you like, you can save it. A color scheme holds information for you about colors of text, background, shadows, and fills. You can save time by re-creating the color scheme you like in new presentations.

Templates create consistency in color and graphic content. Use a ready-made template if you don't have time or interest in deciding which colors to use and where or which graphic elements to include. You can also save your own templates if you like what you've created. Look at the templates in your software and learn from them. You might even take one of them apart and re-create it in a look that pleases you. Keep in mind that less is best and white space is a good thing. The simpler the look, the easier it will be to maintain throughout your slide show. Your audience will appreciate a simple visual message; don't make them try to weed out mentally any unnecessary elements in order to figure out what you're trying to say.

It's easy to change content or revise the order of slides. You can even save different versions of the same file, in order to recall what you presented to group A versus group B.

Animations and slide transitions can give a professional look. Well, sometimes they do. Often, they look hokey. Use them in moderation, and for good reason. Sometimes attention-getting is a good enough reason, but it can't occur frequently because it will defeat its purpose.

Video and photographic images are easy to insert. You can vary the pace and look of your presentation with touches of other media. Be sure to keep video clips short, about the length of a TV commercial. They should enhance and support your presentation. If you need to use a very long video and your equipment isn't the newest, a VCR is the best delivery method. Laptops with DVD will work fine, but not everyone has one.

It is extremely easy to change the order of your presentation. Simply change the view of the "slides" and move them around like cards. If an audience member asks a question covered elsewhere in your presentation, you can go to that slide quickly by jumping to the slide sorter view.

giving an effective computer presentation

Room lighting. Just as with slides, the room must be darkened. Test to see how much room darkening is needed to allow your audience to see. Darken the front of the room and leave as much light on as possible for the audience. Lighter backgrounds often show up better. You'll have to experiment. You might find a big difference between the colors on your computer screen and the colors projected onto the wall screen.

Bells and whistles. You have almost every toy imaginable available to you. Err on the safe side if you are unaccustomed to all of them. Get someone else to look at something if you are unsure that it works well. Make sure the goodies don't detract from your message—they should emphasize your points.

On the other hand…don't just use the computer presentation for all text slides. Give the audience a chance to digest a chart or a photograph that explains your talk in a way that no words could ever do. I've seen many all-text presentations. Not one was memorable; several were pure torture, and I wonder how many were useful.

Speaker notes. The room will be slightly darkened for a computer presentation, so if you will be relying on a binder full of speaker notes, make sure your notes are in a large and readable font. You might need a lectern with a lamp.

Remote slide changes. If you can get the equivalent of a remote control—a wireless mouse—and don't need to rely constantly on speaker notes, you will be more relaxed, since you will be free to move around the room a little.

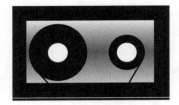

video

We all watch TV so we know that video has some amazing effects.
Done well, video can strongly appeal to emotions or change attitudes,
and the dramatic visual effects can be dazzling. Plus, a video is
consistent. You know the delivery is the same every time. But long
video sequences can be deadly to your presentation: video can lull
people to sleep, or it can seem far more interesting than you! But
video gives you the advantage of a viewpoint other than your own
and, used judiciously, it can be very effective. Clearly, time and expense are most significant with video. If the presentation needs to
really sell an idea or a product and you plan to repeat it often, it is
worth the investment.

Video in small doses. The addition of another voice and point of
view can be refreshing. I gave an educational presentation on confidentiality to medical center staff. I punctuated my remarks with skits
(entertaining particularly because they were enacted by people known
to many in the audience) that depicted a blatant-to-subtle range of
breaches of confidentiality. After each brief video segment, there was
a good discussion of what was wrong and suggestions for more
appropriate actions. Sharing time with the video segments kept
everyone alert and involved.

Speaking of time—long videos are rarely appreciated, unless they're compelling productions. If your aim is to convey information, provide introductory content in another format and use video to present demonstrations or visuals that need animation or drama.

When video must carry the whole message. If you must send a video out in lieu of an in-person presentation, be sure to keep it lively and cinematic. Whose idea was the "talking head"? Avoid it! At the medical center where I worked, we built an enormous outpatient building and lobby that had many features different from the older buildings in the complex. Members of the staff of the medical center needed to get the message about these differences in some consistent and informative fashion. I thought it should be brief and entertaining. My video tour guides were 8- and 10-year old sisters (daughters of an employee) who led us on a ten-minute tour, demonstrating features that differed from the norm along the way, such as call systems, locks, lighting systems, and laundry chutes. Their antics were natural, and the audience was pleased to "see" it before they encountered it. Far better than a dry memo that never got read (although there was additional written information).

working with a video professional

No matter how you use video in your presentation, you'll need to work with someone to get the kind of video you want. Here are some hints for creating a video with the help of a professional:

Impact. Have the impact and outcome firmly in mind. Write down what you want the viewer to experience on emotional and intellectual levels.

Objectives. Write out clear objectives that describe what you want the viewer to learn. (See the appendix section on writing objectives.) You should do this with ANY presentation you create, but you will need to share your objectives with the videographer who can help you translate them to visuals, sound, and motion. Video forces you to define the shortest list of objectives, focused around one main idea. You cannot develop an effective video if you try to include a laundry list of objectives. A good videographer will help you distill your message to achieve the most effective translation to the medium.

Script. Even if you've never written a script for video, give it a try. Divide a lined paper in half lengthwise, and write your audio on the left and what the viewer should see simultaneously on the right. If you don't know what images and sound will work best, write out the messages and emotions you want your viewer to experience. Make it easy for the videographer. If she has to guess at what you want, you won't get what you want.

Trust. Believe the videographer if she tells you that the effect you want will spoil the overall program. Don't try to interfere in the technical aspects of the work. That's why you hired her.

Edit. If you are asked to sit in on the edit, DO! If you're not invited, ask if you can be there. You will have far more creative control, and you'll enjoy seeing it all come together. However, be prepared for long sessions. Editing video takes time. Be polite and defer to the experts—you will need to compromise on some things.

flipcharts

Flipcharts occupy a different place in the presentation spectrum; they are not as visually exciting or compelling as multimedia or video presentations. But we shouldn't ignore flip charts. True, they're often overused or badly used, and it seems as if the rest of the time they're just plain dull. They have their rightful place and they can even be interesting, if you make an effort. Their main advantage is that they're informal, low cost, low tech, easy to produce in an instant, and very little can go wrong (OK, the easel can fall over). Use a flip chart with a small group. Depending on the room, you'll lose people more than thirty feet away.

We're considering the planned use of flip charts—not simply their use in facilitating meetings, although some of the guidelines here will help you produce better ad-hoc flip chart pages. In planned flipchart presentations you will bring in a pad of prewritten pages, just as you would a set of overheads or slides.

some hints for using a flipchart

Write in big, fat, legible letters. Obvious, but it has to be said. We've all sat through informal presentations where we couldn't read a word on the flipchart, either because the writing was small or sloppy or the ink was too light. If letters are not one inch high, they're too small.

Color is good. More is not necessarily better, though. Use color to add meaning, but don't use a rainbow of colors that distract from your message.

White space. I repeat myself because white space gets so little respect!—don't pack presentation media with content in every possible spot. Viewers need some eye relief in the form of white space.

Prepare some charts ahead. Your back faces the audience when you use a flipchart. If you can avoid this situation by working ahead, do it. When you do prepare charts ahead, keep a blank page between them to be sure that the writing on the page behind doesn't show through and distract from your current message.

Cover mistakes with correction ink. Your cover-ups won't be visible to the audience, and you won't have to do it over.

Make cheat notes. If you want the presentation to be dynamic, but also want to make sure that you say everything you intend to say, make some notes on the chart in small letters with a pencil or pen. You'll be the only one who can see them. Or, you can draw in anything you want in pencil and trace over it with marker and look like a real artist to the audience!

Mark pages. Use small, labeled sticky notes like bookmarks to flag pages you want to be able to turn to frequently. Labeling the sticky notes helps in case you need to reveal pages out of their existing order.

Posting pages. If you need to post pages around the room, use sticky flipchart paper or have lots of little strips of tape ready. Just before your presentation, get someone to help you with posting so that you are not interrupted.

Illustrations. Use coloring books for illustrations! I love this idea, from an excellent resource: *Successful Presentations for Dummies*. Coloring books have great, simple drawings that you can trace onto your flipchart for variety. Or you can use an overhead projector to project a simple image from a transparency to the flip chart paper and trace the outline.

Web Sites

What information consumes is rather obvious; it consumes the attention of its recipients. Hence, a wealth of information creates a poverty of attention...

Herbert A. Simon

Providing a section on Web sites is probably foolhardy because this is the only section of this book that could be outdated in a week. But I will forge ahead because, for many (myself included), using the Web can still be a frustrating experience. Your browser had better be the latest version, or some sites will look scrambled. Even if you have all the latest hardware and software, it can still pose a challenge. Making it easy and fun to get to needed information is what it's all about. There are resources with excellent technical advice, a few of which are listed in the reference section. The discussion here will concentrate on the visual approach and on content. Start by thinking through what your user wants and needs.

what users ask

I like Jennifer Fleming's list of basic questions in the minds of users when they navigate the Web (she wrote *Web Navigation: Designing the User Experience*):

1   **Where am I?** Give the visitor an idea of where he is in your site. At a minimum, provide a link to a site map; site maps are often nothing more than a list of links. If at all possible, offer a view of the entire site from the first page. Amazon.com uses the tab metaphor—the

---

outermost tab is the page you are "on." Other sites indicate the current page by highlighting it on the menu of page choices. There are many elegant solutions. Have a look at some Web design sites to see samples.

2   **Where can I go?** Links aren't often sufficiently descriptive. It is helpful to provide rollovers that cause a text box to appear in a consistent location containing more detail about the link's content. (If that detail consists of a submenu of associated links, they had better be clear to the user. Test a few representative audience members.) It's terribly daunting to get to a site with a long list of links and no descriptions of what can be found by taking them. People want to be able to make an informed decision before embarking on the journey to a new site that might take a bit of time to load and end up boring or useless.

3   **How will I get there?** Navigational aids should be as unobtrusive and clear as can be. A site map is important if you have a complicated site. Navigating the Web operates on the same principles as navigating the grocery store or a large building complex. I developed a wayfinding program for patients of a sprawling medical center that resolved at least some of the confusion over where to park, where to enter, and which path to follow. Think about being sick and unable to find your doctor's office in an enormous complex. That would make anyone sicker. What was done? Patients were given both standardized and specific information on cards mailed to them as a reminder, prior to their scheduled appointment. Cards had maps of the building and parking areas, written directions to the clinical department, the phone number for the area, address, and a fill-in space for the doctor's name and appointment time. People actually did bring them along. When they did, if they made a mistake, took a wrong turn or parked in the wrong lot, any employee in the medical center (who quickly became familiar with the cards) could help.

So patients had clear, available information with a sense of expectation of what was to come. And there was a plethora of navigational assistance, should patients enter through one of the many available "wrong" doors. On the Web, people can easily enter a site through a "back" door. If they have no clue as to where they're going, or if there's nothing to help them to get to your menu of what's available, you will lose them or make them mad.

4   **How can I get back to where I once was?** Once a user finds a good spot on your site, give him clues about finding his way back. Give him familiar signposts or a menu of choices to get back to the index (home) page, or to a page with clear links.

what do users hate?

I really like Jennifer Fleming's list of user pet peeves. I'll bet you could list most of them: waiting, going where they didn't want to go, getting lost, having to download some plug-in, and pages that are hard to read. I have a couple of additions to the list: Web sites that give no indication of the phone, email, or address information anywhere. What are they trying to hide? And pop-up windows. Usually they include advertising and frequently they open any time you go back to a certain page. Closing pages you never wanted to open can be irritating. New annoyances are created regularly, so this list is bound to expand.

I've been a guilty Web-builder: my first Web site was pretty, but full of Java and took time to load. Back then Java wasn't common, and the site looked like gobbledygook to users on all but the newest browsers. Great advertising for me. But the lessons aren't hard to learn. Keep it simple and clear, test it under every possible condition, and have lots of people test drive it and give you the horrible truth.

One simple way to make sure your site can be viewed clearly, as you intend it to be seen, is to keep the overall size like that of **the lowest-resolution monitors.** It does leave some empty space for the folks with higher-resolution monitors, but it's worth it not to discourage your audience. If you create a masterpiece for the high-resolution monitor, you will be in for a rude surprise when your friend calls you to say he can't read a darn thing.

Another way to ensure your site looks right to users is to anticipate the use of **old versions of browsers.** Most people don't update browsers frequently because downloading takes time and the benefits aren't always clear. I'm not advocating developing for prehistoric versions of browsers, on the other hand. But some happy middle ground will keep your audience from becoming grumpy.

There are several sites, such as killersites.com, where you can view the **best of the Web.** I encourage you to do so; it's fun and instructive. I hesitate to offer examples of truly horrible Web sites, but Vincent Flanders and Michael Willis, coauthors of *Web Pages That Suck* (at webpagesthatsuck.com), have no such reservations. The commentary is amusing and you will learn something.

how do you make it easy on users?

In summary, just as with any document you create, there are things you can do:

— Provide a **clear path** for the user's eye to follow. The same design principles from previous chapters apply here.

— Make **navigation obvious.** What's obvious? You need to give the user an idea of what is behind the link BEFORE she actually takes it. Provide more information about the link than necessary, so that the user is making a conscious choice. Let users know where they've been, too.

— Keep the **text minimal** and easy to read. That's not always possible if you are creating a news site where people are reading content online. But you can set up the full text of each article on a page of its own to keep distractions to a minimum. Computer screens are not wonderful for reading long passages.

— **Don't go crazy** with techno-wizardry that will be lost on the people who haven't upgraded their software and equipment in the past year.

— Keep the **embellishments to a minimum.** You want it to be interesting but, as Edward Tufte says (quoting Pugin), you can "decorate construction but never construct decoration." The focus should

stay on your information. If you can make it clearer, make it stand
out as it should, great. Adding frills will not help the cause. (By the
way, if you do get a copy of *Envisioning Information*, on page 34 you
will see the picture of a building shaped like a duck. It's a great example of constructing decoration and funny, in a sad way.)

design and implementation considerations

Not surprisingly, the fundamental principles and elements of design
apply to the Web. However, some differences from general design
principles lie in the pressure to offer technical wonders and in the
possibility for user-interaction.

Analysis is always a handy first step. What do you want the site to
do, and who will be visiting? Begin to **create a model of user actions** and what the site will do in response. A site that makes heavy
use of databases will require the expertise of a Web developer. But
you can think through a simpler site via storyboarding, before you
begin even one line of code. You can define the core functionality of
your site and establish overall navigation and locations where users
will enter.

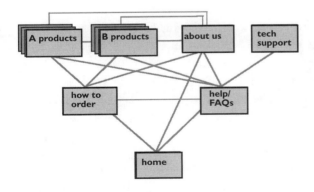

a simple, graphic dimensional storyboard

The exercise of creating a graphic display (on paper) of your site is valuable for keeping the navigation between content areas clear in your mind, particularly if you are the visual type. It becomes a kind of dimensional storyboard, giving you an immediate sense of relationships. The storyboard/site map shown on page 273 depicts the hypothetical user's current location, or recent link, highlighted. In this example, only from "help/FAQs" can the user get to "tech support." He has to view canned help before requesting technical support. And, maybe the reason tech support is not available from every page is to keep the techs from becoming inundated with the simple stuff.

Create your storyboard in 3-x-5-inch cards. Add information behind each card as you determine content for an area. Use coded numbers to describe a "branch" of the site. For example: in the storyboard shown, "1-Home" to "2-How to Order" to "3-A Products" would constitute a branch and the numbers connote the number of pages into the site the user must penetrate to see this content. You can lay the cards on a table in front of you, as if you were giving a Tarot reading, and move them around as you think things through. More experienced Web designers might think this is overkill. When you're new at it, it works.

So you have thought through what you want your visitor to see first and what you want him to see next, and after that. You're establishing that visual hierarchy. Consider the reaction you want to get. Make the flow of information lead the visitor to your conclusion. This becomes more complex when you consider each page is a point of entry to your site. People will find your site through a page other than home. Make it easy for them to get to the location of most interest.

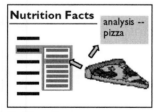

Rolling the mouse over a selection opens up a text box revealing more information about the link.

Everyone wants to know exactly where he is going BEFORE clicking on that link. Many sites employ mouseovers that cause a text box to appear describing the content of the link, to help visitors decide whether or not to continue.

A flaw of many Web sites, in fact, a flaw of many organizations, is their insistence upon the users or customers learning their structure or operations. Not an overt insistence, simply a disregard for the user's viewpoint and failure to organize things from that viewpoint. You know how all of your data are structured, but before you create a final navigational design for your site, get some advice from a typical user. What would he want to find if he visited your site? And how would he want to find it?

Special effects and animation. Do you think that you have to have toys to play with and special effects to keep users occupied? Consider the number of people using old browsers; if you lock them out of your site, you might lose a large number of potential users. Or, if you think you must have a flashy "movie" intro to your site, you could be turning away people who might otherwise have been interested in the content you offer. However, if you know your audience is looking to you to provide leading edge stuff, do so!

How will your audience respond to moving images? If you must use them, be sure they have a purpose. Jakob Nielsen describes the use of animation in detail, and there is a rich range. He even includes attracting attention as a **legitimate use of animation.** If link-rot were not a problem, it would be wonderful to provide URLs that illustrate good uses of animation. You've seen some of them:

— map sites where zooming permits a more detailed view of the map

— "time-lapse" style illustrations

— a three-dimensional product from a variety of perspectives, sometimes with user control of the view

If you believe your content requires the use of animation—and animation shouldn't be superfluous—consult experts, like Nielsen.

Interaction. I hesitated to use the word interactivity. It means something different to everyone. For some, it means merely playing with content. For others, it means a site begins to "know" its users and customizes content for them (through the use of cookies and unique IDs or some other device). Providing interaction and activities can certainly enhance user involvement and that means users will stay around longer. But interaction is not just about supplying toys, games, links, or video. Nothing's wrong with games and fun, if that's the intent of your site! Real interaction is about engaging the user. Be sure your site warrants this kind of "engagement." Interactivity for its own sake is worse than no interactivity; often, people are truly browsing and want to gather information quickly and go on.

Engage users in something meaningful. My goal is for people to learn something when using sites I create, so I make sure there are opportunities to interact with other people, conduct research and share findings, solve a problem together, work on a project together, and so on. I find interaction with other people most effective and engaging, but it is possible to get people involved in online activity that does not involve direct communication with other users. Invite them to interact with the content by solving a puzzle and comparing the solution to those of other users. Conduct an online poll. You can make it fun and get their brains involved, too!

getting it done

Seek the experts for highly technical considerations. You might choose to use a Web design application or hire the technical work out. If you use an application, you will have a number of templates and ready-made graphics to choose from to speed up the creation of the site. However, chances are the templates available won't be what you have in mind, and you will be on your own, and perhaps stuck, when a problem arises. Your time to solve problems will become costly. If you work with a technical person, the hourly cost will become a factor, and you might need to scale back your original concept. A compromise? Organize all content first, then create a storyboard, and finally create some rough HTML pages. Then hire a technical person to do the things you can't do, like polish the pages, troubleshoot, establish navigation, check it in multiple browsers and platforms, and help with the registration.

Even if you do none of the technical work of preparing the site, you should be actively involved in defining it: assembling content, determining categories, roughing out a storyboard, mapping out an architecture, assessing the preliminary design, and testing the final design prior to launch. The guidelines that follow will help you assess the work done.

Text. Use it judiciously. The Web is primarily visual; people have low tolerance for reading large text documents from a computer screen. This may change in just a few years, but until that happens a downloadable PDF for large documents is often appreciated.

Having said that the Web is not the best place for heavy use of text, I do not mean to imply that all your text content should be short phrases, bullet lists, or two-sentence paragraphs. The best sites provide an organized selection of links to follow to a choice of content. If link selections are categorized and annotated where necessary the user can make a decision about which one to follow. The Springer Spaniel News Network depicts a simplified example:

A way to organize a text-heavy site

Line length. Just as with a paper document, individual lines of text cannot be overly long. And the longer the line of text is, the more space (leading) you'll need to add between lines to make the text readable. Computer screens are not the greatest place for reading. Use the line length guidelines for print documents and see if that works. Rather than reading text carefully, people generally try to scan text on the Web; you might want to shorten lines further to permit faster scanning.

Type. There are those who believe that serif-style type works best on the Web, just as it does on paper. My own online preference is for the cleaner lines of sans-serif type. Often, the screen renders the serifs badly. Experiment and then view the results on a different browser and different computer. If you are content with the default type, usually Arial and Times Roman, it's easy. If not, you (or your technical assistant) can use font-control tags, or define styles with downloadable fonts.

Language is an important issue. Database creators use a "controlled vocabulary." The phone book's yellow pages provides an example: try looking up 'hair stylist' and you might be redirected to 'barbers' and 'beauty salons.' A specified word is used to describe a topic. If your site will have a search function, you will need to be rigorous in ensuring that searchers retrieve information successfully. Even with no search function, simple ease of navigation requires consistent terminology, what database creators call "naming conventions," to help users find their way through your site. Labeling needs to be brief, clear, and consistent. For example, it could be mildly disquieting for a user to follow a link to a 'survey' and find the content there labeled 'questionnaire.'

Search capability within a site is sometimes expected, but it requires database know-how. Sites with complex content will benefit from a search function available on the navigation bar. People visit the Web for information and search functions promise to get them quickly to the information they seek. Unless otherwise specified, users will assume the entire site is searched.

Make your site visible. Speaking of search capability, you want to make sure users can find your site in the first place if you're going to devote the energy to creating one. Meta-tags within the HTML of the page header are the most common way to ensure that you have some key words to describe your site. Register with the most popular search engines.

Navigation cannot be overly stressed. The organization and structure of your site must be clear and consistent. An easy approach to ensuring that your site structure is clear for your audience is to keep the same navigational strip, with links to home and major content areas, available no matter where someone lands in the site. They know they can always get back to a familiar location.

Jakob Nielsen advises using page titles that convey the overall message of the page as a navigational aid. In fact, Nielsen's own site makes use of a clear page title in the highly useful navigation bar:

useit.com ➡ alertbox ➡ **July 2000 End of Web Design**

This navigation bar is always at the top of the page and the last item listed, which is not underlined, indicates the current page. It's easy to select the link to visit a previous page. (I chose this selection because it offers an interesting perspective on Web design.) This type of navigation is called "breadcrumbs" because it allows the user to find her way back along the path she took to get to the current location. If your site will have deep layers of content, this is an elegant solution. If your site will be shallow in structure, having a breadth of links from one main page, you can provide multiple links from your home page, as in Example B on page 287.

Frames allow visits to other, even unrelated, sites while keeping the navigational strip available. Frames also have disadvantages—for example, your audience cannot bookmark specific pages in frames, many browsers cannot print frame pages, and search engines might not reference frame pages correctly. Most of the authorities, such as Jacob Nielsen, strongly recommend against frames, but Jennifer Fleming has some excellent advice on their use.

If you decide against frames, you can try pop-up windows or tabs (see Example A, page 285). Don't overuse pop-up windows; they can be annoying. If you go with tabs made to look like file folders, be sure that your content always appears within the context of its respective tab category. If the tab disappears with one click into the content on a tab page, the purpose of the tab is defeated because the user no longer knows which "file folder" he is in. Consider too, users who visit your site and land on a page other than the home page. These visitors should have some idea of the context of the site, and the name of the page should be clear.

A **site map, or guide to your site,** is a way to reveal to the audience where they are, or where they can go, within your site. By all means ensure that the home page incorporates the full guide to your site; that's ideal. But if your home page cannot explain the site fully, a site map, or index, must be available because people will land on your site anywhere—not necessarily the home page. Graphic site maps, similar to the example of a storyboard for designing a Web site, are rarely done, but a text-based index on your home page, with many categories of information, can be effectively done with an expandable/collapsible outline of contents. All listings should link to their corresponding locations.

Back to **links.** It can be terribly <u>distracting</u> to land on a site with an interesting bit of <u>text</u> chock full of <u>hypertext</u> inviting you to go <u>elsewhere</u>. Consider using one <u>link</u> to a <u>glossary</u> or to a series of links at the bottom of the page and only a few links within the main body of the text. You see lines full of hypertext everywhere. The much-touted goal is to keep visitors within your own site as much as possible (although that goal is questionable if part of the value your site provides is references to more content!). If the links are to definitions, you might provide a glossary link instead, to reduce the frustration of reading narrative with multiple invitations to read something else. Or, create text boxes that appear on mouseover; this is a less obtrusive way to offer the information and it doesn't give your reader the impression that you think she needs definitions.

If you have lots of links on your site, you can make sure users know where the links are taking them by providing a rich context. Instead of a laundry list, provide categories of links. Or provide a set of tabs to pages for major groupings of content. Instead of extra Web pages for short content, provide text boxes that appear and disappear with no more user effort than moving the mouse. Get the user to the content he wants with a minimum of clicking.

Link colors. Most of the references on navigation I've read insist that unvisited links should be blue in color, while visited links should be red or purple. I absolutely agree that you should make sure the color is different for visited and unvisited hypertext links. I absolutely disagree with the idea that the blue/red color scheme is now a classic, expected aspect of Web navigation. (Many years ago I took a spreadsheet class with an instructor who insisted that VisiCalc, while by then a relic, was a classic. Even though better programs were available, we would learn VisiCalc. What?) I think people pick up on the color scheme for a site pretty quickly and will not be thrown by gold links that change to brown once visited, as long is the change is consistent. Blue, red, and purple link colors might not fit every color scheme and I rebel against this meaningless tyranny.

Graphics and sound are known memory hogs. Bouncing and noisy animations that never stop distract. I don't have the patience to wait for a page or file to load. Simple graphics that take no time to load are still not universal on the Web. It is surprising how many sites force a wait for loading, even with a cable modem or DSL. Apparently, people think their flashy demonstrations are worth waiting for; lots of users don't. And there are still people out there using the standard phone connection; you have to consider them. We hope that in the very near future everyone will have more bandwidth and everyone can stop yelling about this.

Keep graphic files small by cropping images and by using JPEG file format for photos and GIF format for nonphoto graphics. Allow the audience to control what they view by clicking on thumbnail images when they want to view the full-size image. Interlaced GIFs, which look like Venetian blinds while loading (common in the days of really-slow-load-time) permit the visitor to see a vague preview of the image to come and to make a decision about waiting. You can also specify the precise height and width of an image, which allows the browser to paint text around the area where the picture will load; your visitor can read while the download is underway.

Sound file capabilities, once very crude and slow, have improved immensely. However, allow your visitor to control what he hears, to save time and to prevent forcing an unwelcome sound on him; amazingly, there are lots of sites builders who think they know the type of music or sound effects you want to hear! If you use sound, make sure it is integral to the purpose of your site. For example, the site I created for a vocal group contains sound files the user can choose to hear. Also, you must be aware of the large deaf audience making great use of the Web; if you deliver critical information via sound files, you will miss this group. If your message is international (the Web is World Wide, after all) you may miss another audience.

On the Web, technical problems can sabotage the best information design. If you have no technical help, take advantage of one of the many online site "doctors" that will, for no fee, at least check your site for broken links and evaluate graphics for download efficiency.

If you are using clip art or other graphics that you did not create, be sure to check on **copyrights** to avoid a legal problem. Web sites with graphics and clip art generally post their policy for use. If you are creating the graphics, keep them simple and use Web safe colors.

Backgrounds, really fancy ones, are still in use in lots of Web sites. They can really frustrate a reader if they contain complex patterns that interfere with legibility. If you are tempted to incorporate a complex background—think again. Is it worth adding load time and decreasing legibility? Black on soft off-white, or a muted shade, is an admittedly tame but easy to read option. If that sounds too hideously boring, add splashes of saturated colors around the sides. If a background interferes at all with your message, get a new one (background, I mean).

Wild or neon colors don't provide a suitable background for text either. It might look cool the moment you create it, but the chances are the audience partial to lime-green backgrounds is small. Review the rules Tufte cites for the use of color on page 105. When you get really, really good, you can start breaking the rules.

Structuring the individual page involves a number of decisions. Look at some sites and decide what you do and do not like. I think many home pages look too crowded. White space doesn't have to be white, it just needs to be there. You can't direct a visitor's eye if you have a page crammed with text, links, and competing graphics. There are sites that have lots of links on the home page, but they're organized in categories, colors, tabs, and so on. The viewer doesn't have to do the sorting. So I'm not saying that you must avoid complexity, simply that you need to handle it well. With complexity comes a need for more layout skill to preserve clarity.

There is often a good reason to have a great deal of information at the "front door" of a site. If visitors arrive at your site and can't be sure if the site will answer their questions, they're likely to go away. That's the argument people make when they see that my home page has only a few links to the content within. But my rationale is that people going to my site are likely to be holding my business card, or have read an article I wrote, and are already interested in what might be inside. I'm not providing more than a brochure of content for people without a password to the conference area. So I know my site's not "sticky," but I don't want to put in the effort to keep it constantly engaging, because I have other work to do. Using the Web to work with my clients—that's worth my time.

The information you provide at the front door or home page of your site should be just what the users are looking for. Instead of telling them about your mission and vision statements and how long you've been in business, give them choices that reflect what typical customers want. Maybe they DO want to know about your vision; you can offer them the option to read it.

Review the section on **grids.** Use a grid as the basis for your layout, just as you would with a paper document. Your viewer needs visual clues to be able to predict where information will be found throughout the site. The difference here is in the frustrating limitations of HTML. You don't have the freedom to do everything you want. The grid's importance is even greater in Web sites, because you want the viewer to feel as though he knows exactly where he is on a page.

Use **tables** to keep things in position on a Web page. The table is invisible to the viewer (with borders set to zero) but keeps the content in one section from bleeding into another or just spreading out onto the whole screen.

Screen size is an important consideration. A screen of information on the computer is smaller than a normal sheet of 8.5-x-11-inch paper, and a viewer might not scroll to see the full content. Also, your viewer might have a small monitor.

You can set up lots of heading styles in HTML. But you don't want to burden your viewer with too many cues to remember. The visual hierarchy you set up should be clear very quickly, so try to use only a few heading styles. Set up a **style sheet,** just as you would with a paper document, and stick to it. Decide what headings and subheadings will look like and the spacing between lines and paragraphs. Consistency will make your site a pleasure to navigate.

About ensuring **consistency;** it's essential on the Web. The user should be able to get to different information and locations on the site in similar ways. A simple example is keeping the navigation bar in the same location. But, frankly, the navigation bar is usually a big target so it's less likely to be a problem to find. It's the little things that frustrate users: on one page, I click on this icon, and it takes me to another spot on the same page, on another page the same icon takes me to a different page. Or, I click on the link entitled "search" and land on a page called "data query."

That brings us to **maintenance,** which MUST be done. Don't build anything bigger than you want to maintain or pay someone to maintain. Out-of-date content and broken links are exasperating to visitors and costly to your credibility.

home page layouts

The fairly standard examples shown here are not the best of the Web by any means! Just examples to make you think about what you like before you build it. According to Jakob Nielsen, too many sites are over-designed, taking too long to load and making viewing from small, hand-held devices very difficult. I see his point, every day on the Web! And yet I wonder if the Web might become a bit boring when all sites are plain text with few graphics. An effort is involved in visiting a Web site, so some enticement is useful. Make your site original but keep the implementation as simple as possible.

You could set up your page symmetrically with text or key content in the middle and optional sidebars or graphic items at the sides, with the title and tabs for regular site locations at the top, like example A:

Example A

grid – Example A

Each page would follow a similar grid set-up. The tab metaphor is one way to handle the "where am I?" question. (Like any other structural metaphor, it has many detractors.) The breadcrumbs navigational technique would be an excellent, and simpler, alternative. The illustrations indicated at the sides could change, giving you flexibility with content, such as advertising. Don't forget to leave blank space at the side for those viewing on a low resolution monitor.

One caution. If you like things centered PLEASE left-justify longer passages of text; centered text has a rather random look and is a challenge to read. It's OK to center a table of information with short entries, like a list of seating areas in a theatre next to their corresponding prices, or the glossary of this book.

Any number of layouts is valid, as long as there is some consistency among pages. While tables and HTML, even DHTML and Java, can be limiting, you do have options. Lots of sites are making very creative use of tables. Early on, the simple asymmetrical layout with a navigational bar on the left became a classic:

Example B

For some sites, only eight links on the home page would be frustratingly few if you need to have everything possible available at the point of entry to your site (for example, showing the full list of orchids, rather than major categories). If you will have lots of links to content, give the viewer some focal points and a clear way to distinguish the areas of interest from the areas to ignore. Include some space around elements. It is hard enough to read text on a screen; a zillion links in a teeny-weeny font will force people to give up quickly, particularly if they link to other unknown locations.

Each page in such a site would show the main navigational links at the left side. The links shown at the bottom could be used for more static information. One often sees the "contact us," "glossary," "company information," or "site map" in less prominent locations separate from the more dynamic content at the left. Or, the main links are often repeated in text form at the bottom of the page to ensure that all browsers can render the important navigation. Again, that gray area should not have text—giant or small—spanning the entire width. (My example does, I know! But I don't have a small enough font. Giant letters that look like that would be stupid on the Web.) Text on the Web needs to be easy to scan. So break it up with graphics or text in columns, depending upon the content. If you must place text in front of a graphic, be sure it's readable. The Orchid example is a little hard to read here in gray tones.

grid – Example B

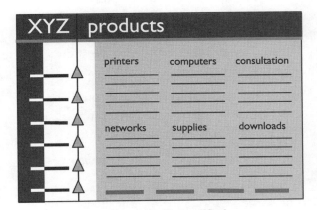

Example B, modified

Handling lots of content. The modified version of Example B is loosely based on the previous grid. This is a site with gobs of links (gobs for the purpose of this oversimplified illustration) right on the main or home page. Note that links are categorized, so that your reader doesn't have to spend time slogging through deep lists of unrelated content, scrolling through one long list, or making wild guesses. Each link might actually be a pull-down menu of choices within that smaller category.

Here is a distinct advantage the Web offers: your visitor can probe for whatever depth of information is available on your site by drilling down to the detail. The XYZ company offers a simple example. If your visitor can quickly find a printer brand, then a model, then a subclass of the model, then the specific class of supplies he needs, such as cartridges, and finally the specific cartridge he wants to buy, you will earn his respect and his repeat business. Even more impressive are sites that, through a series of screening questions, take the visitor to a specific troubleshooting decision tree that helps her decide whether a call to a technician is in order, or whether she can make an adjustment herself. In sites like this the selections seem natural to the user, and he gets to his goal efficiently. Sites that remember user history and preferences provide added value.

Some cautions about organizing with lots of categories:
— Don't do it unless the categories can be universally understood. People will get frustrated trying to find the item they want in all those scroll boxes. But you can provide a depth of exploration of the information behind those links.

— Be sure the categories are of interest to users. What do users want to see? If they rarely order certain supplies, perhaps that category needs to be deleted, or maybe you should market them differently.

— Ensure that the hierarchy of information behind each category is as consistent as possible.

Handling long lists or narrative text. What if your site will display lots of information, as in a long list or narrative text? You have choices: you can show the entire list or narrative in one long, scrolling marathon. Or, you can divide it up into separate pages, but make them fast-loading or people on slow connections won't be happy. Better yet, if the list can be outlined with categories and subcategories, you can make it collapsible/expandible; the user will only see the content of interest at any one time.

Another option. A more casual shopping site might use a drop-down menu—with a click on the category, the subcategories appear. A click on the specific item, and a corresponding screen of information with a graphic appears. Opens up some white space on the screen and the possibility of illustrations. Good Web design allows the user to probe precisely what he wants to view, without distraction. And good Web design doesn't force the user to look in a number of locations, without success, before finding what she wants.

Drop-down menus save space and permit visitors to focus on one thing at a time.

Testing must be done in every browser and on the major platforms. Try to get a half-dozen typical audience members with different machines and browsers to view your site for you. At least one will see something mildly horrifying—either in your layout/design or in problems with the way the site is rendered on her monitor. I learned the hard way, running our first Web-based focus groups. We ended up doing a redesign, because AOL couldn't handle cascading windows, among other things. We test thoroughly on AOL now. If you are setting up a commercial site, hire an outside testing company, since any errors will be very costly to you. If you put the time and money into designing and implementing a site, you want it to look and act exactly as you plan. Get ready for some change and compromise, or you'll never launch your dot-com, dot-org, or dot-whatever.

> Apply this Web site checklist to a few of your favorite sites. How well did they meet the criteria?
>
> - **Layout** based on a grid
> - **Content** is concise, of high quality, with appropriate "shelf-life"
> - **Visual hierarchy** apparent
> - **Labeling** is consistent
> - **Controlled vocabulary**
> - **Navigation** is logical, apparent
> - **Links** provide clues about their destination

using the Web effectively

The Web is the most dimensional form of information design, where many fields play an important role: computer science and information technology, communication arts, graphic design, psychology, and instruction.

Content

Web sites range from scholarly exchange to pure entertainment. Web gurus everywhere say that you must constantly update your content (to mention a few, Jakob Nielsen, author of *Designing Web Usability,* or Vincent Flanders and Michael Willis, coauthors of *Web Pages That Suck*). I know I've said I don't spend lots of time updating information for the casual browser, but I actually do keep my capability statement, publication list, newsletter, conference area, and client sites up-to-date. As Flanders and Willis would say, if you don't have any content, why build a site at all?

Jakob Nielsen recommends using at least half, and preferably much more, of the real estate on a Web page for content. However, he also states that people simply scan content for a number of reasons: reading from a computer screen is more difficult than reading a paper document; there are multiple distractions to lead users to other locations; and, they can't afford the time to read everything thoroughly. Therefore, content should be distilled to its essence and crystal clear. If a glance at your home page doesn't give a clear indication of what the site contains, if it doesn't represent your organization (or product or whatever you are describing there) accurately, you have rework to do. Divide content into categories that users can probe more deeply.

Content is often treated as something provided to others. Interaction has often been envisioned as users playing with bells and whistles. Fortunately, this is changing rapidly. Due to its unique features, the Web is becoming a powerful social and communication environment, with users allowed to participate in content building. Users hold a great deal of useful information. Capturing this tacit information requires a new approach. Rather than placing simply interactive content on the Web, users can become information providers.

the communication environment

I often use my Web site to communicate with clients—showing them documents in progress, or a project status report. Posting documents on the Web permits multiple people to provide input. One relatively new feature is the use of what I call (for lack of a technical term) online **"sticky-notes,"** the online equivalent to the 3M product. None of the original documents is changed, so the writer can feel certain the version is the original, but the "sticky-notes" added by each editor describe the changes or additions they want. Plus, editors can read one another's notes, so the writer won't see the same edit multiple times. The writer can take responsibility for the final resolution, posting revised versions until consensus is achieved; this can save many hours of hair-pulling and bad words. There are even more robust versions of document collaboration in which users can propose and "vote" upon changes and additions to content.

A project **schedule** posted online is a good way to make sure everyone is aware of events. A fully implemented project site with links to threaded discussions, logs of activities, and archived project information will require significantly more effort. Someone—a facilitator familiar with the project—will have to be responsible for **archiving old discussions, summarizing** important points to ensure the integrity of the repository of information about project history, milestone events, and current status.

Discussion areas within an electronic conference allow participants to share information, create a body of knowledge, report status and ask for help. Once a decision is made or a deliverable is completed, the inactive discussion area can be deleted. If a history will be maintained, a brief summary of each discussion section will suffice. This history will help trace where a project might have gone off-track or document how to do something right. Either way, you stand to make performance improvements based on the history's availability.

Clearly, the next step from such uses of the Web—for service support, for customer comment, for project activity—is to use it as a knowledge repository. A discussion area, dynamic and changing in its content, can form the precursor to a **knowledge repository,** which takes on a more formal, structured, and permanent form. Someone has to take responsibility for organizing, summarizing, and archiving the volumes of information, because a working site needs to be clear and engaging—never overwhelming! People should be able to probe the depths but should not be faced with a massive quantity of information at one time. The repository can be a convenient way to learn from the successes and failures of others.

With all of the rapidly increasing technological options we have, it is best to use only what you need and disregard unnecessary forays into distracting and complicated technology. Mauri Collins and Zane Berge coined the term "technological minimalism," referring to using the lowest level of technology required to achieve an objective. Use the simplest tool that will work and you will ensure greater participation and far less frustration and failure.

make it easy for learners

Support e-learning
process by providing:

- Integrated content
- Structure
- Interaction with
     facilitator/faculty
     other students
     experts
     content
- Feedback
- Evaluation

Indeed, the Web has become the hot place for learning. Unfortunately, most commercial implementations of Web-based course management systems, and I've used several, still don't yet make it easy on the learner! (I am talking about systems that deliver learning, not learning management systems that administer overall organizational training.) I hope, since I'm involved in online learning as a designer and instructor, that what I complain about here becomes obsolete rapidly with the burgeoning interest. But some of the most widely used commercial course management systems have inflexible structures, dividing content into "exercises," "readings," "discussion," "documents," and so on. With a structure like that, the learner has to put it all together himself; he has to do extra work to find out which reading goes with which assignment. E-learning should allow the user to view content related to specific learning objectives in context. **Integration of content** only makes sense.

With respect to **content:** yes, it is critical to have accurate and meaningful content in any information you provide. However, textbook material posted online might look flashier, but it won't enhance the learning process. This has lead some to conclude that learning technology is just an expensive fad. There are ways to build in the features that aid the learner in higher forms of education. We can't blame the technology if our use of it is the real problem.

What is needed for quite a bit of subject matter is a **social context.** While people can learn the basics of spreadsheet software with a self-contained computer-based approach, I don't know of a way to teach philosophy or English composition without facilitation of some sort.

Incredibly, many systems still force the learner and facilitator to log in to check for changes, often to be disappointed that the effort was for nothing! It's akin to picking up the phone to answer it when it's not ringing. Instead, participants should receive some kind of **notification,** most likely through email, of significant new postings! People probably will not put up with logging in with no payoff for long.

The technology being developed for learning holds great promise, but its application toward learning so far is weak. The current technology focuses on organizing and presenting content, but it should do more to support the learner in exploring the learning objectives, to support the effective mentoring dialogue between instructor and learner, to support teams of learners in demonstrating their mastery of the content, and to support the instructor in assessing the learner's mastery of the learning objectives.

Components of a knowledge repository should be readily accessible, available to enhance performance. These items have grown from the discussion, from experience, and from the organizing and summarizing of the facilitator:

— Archives and summaries of previous discussion about the topics

— Discussion area for investigators of the content where experts may be invited to join in

— Static materials, such as:

- Actual scenarios, simulations, case studies, and lessons learned
- Articles, reference works, and participant files
- Practice tools, such as games
- Directions, references, syllabi
- Performance-support guidance and job aids
- Self-assessment tools and study guides
- Lists of experts/mentors and how to contact them
- Related Web sites

The last component of any learning repository is the social and emotional component, which is the most valuable to the experience. As I complained before, anyone can put some files on the Web and call it a course. But, to facilitate discovery through simulations, project-based learning, problem-solving, and hands-on approaches takes a great effort. The reward is equally great. Create a social space for collaborative learning and people will be motivated to participate because they will learn something there!

People can work and learn productively together in the online environment, collaborating and sharing information. Working and learning should occur simultaneously; they are not two separate endeavors, but part of a continuum. What has been missing in the mix is the connection between the classroom and collective repository of knowledge residing in policy, procedure, experience, and expertise. Building the repository becomes a recursive process, integral to the life of the organization and to the learning of its members. What better basis for an e-learning system than the knowledge gathered and refined from the repository?

building the repository

How do you ensure a repository is useful, for learning and for creating a reference resource? Structure the input to organize it, appoint a facilitator or librarian to manage the information, and ensure that experienced people verify the information.

Structure the input: In any situation where user participation is encouraged, input must be structured to ensure that it is consistent. Use a menu approach, such as **pull-down** lists or **radio-button** selection lists, when the information expected from users can be selected from a discrete set of values. Text boxes encourage more free-form contributions, but you can structure these contributions by posing specific questions and providing guidance about length and content.

You can make it fun for users at the same time. Everyone appreciates seeing data provided by others. For example, offer instant **polling** with results that change the moment a "vote" is cast. That's a simple implementation. Build upon the voting by allowing users to vote on the helpfulness of other users' contributions. This method is in use in some online retail systems and service-support systems. You've seen the ratings of book reviews on Amazon.com.

Appoint a facilitator/librarian: In a class situation, the instructor assumes both roles. However, people should be encouraged to con-

---

Roles needed to ensure a useful repository

Facilitator role

- encourage participation
- provide feedback
- organize input
- review input
- update information

Librarian role

- verify submissions
- summarize content
- categorize content
- archive content

INFORMATION DESIGN DESK REFERENCE

tribute at any time, and a facilitator is needed to encourage participation, provide feedback, organize the input and gather more where needed. The facilitator takes on a librarian role when summarizing, cataloging, and archiving content of a repository. The facilitator determines which submissions require verification by an expert before they are archived.

The facilitator can add topics to the repository that include uploaded reference material. On our own site, each topic automatically generates its own discussion area where the facilitator poses questions and problems and asks follow-up questions based on participant responses. Discussion participants often identify new reference material and suggest different topics. In a typical scenario, a participant cites an interesting article in a discussion comment. The facilitator reviews the article to determine the value of the content to the entire user population. If the article is valuable, the facilitator adds the article to the content, and he might create a new discussion area.

Utilize experienced people as verifiers: Certain new submissions, particularly in mission critical areas, require the attention of experienced people, experts, who can determine whether they are correct or not. This is peer review with veto power (or with the power to emphasize a particularly important entry!). It has to happen for people to trust the data.

As an example, service technicians in some companies are responsible to update a Web database of service help information with their own contributions and evaluations of other contributions. An expert verifies the information and decides whether or not to incorporate it into the core repository. This is all made possible because the Web is widely available and instantly updateable.

using the Web differently

To give you an **example** of a different use of the Web from the standard site: we developed an application to support Web-based focus groups and surveys for medical research, corporate decision-making, project communication, and other uses. The option of anonymous dialogue provides for uses such as 360-degree feedback or other sensitive discussions supporting research, management, and information gathering on a number of levels.

Threaded discussions are asynchronous, but the browser refreshes every thirty seconds, permitting those online simultaneously to view one another's comments as they are added. Discussions are viewable online as a threaded outline, full transcript, or hybrid of the two. Anyone can post a question to the discussion area that solicits a formal poll of the group (i.e., the message can specify a discrete set of options from which others may select). A display of the original message shows an immediate tally of responses. It's a simple implementation, easy to use, and valuable to the users who create the content.

the future

The newest use of the online environment is not pushing information at hapless users (although that is done, often offensively). Instead, my hope is that new systems of information flow will complete a loop: discoveries and innovations of users will be reviewed and evaluated by experts and then incorporated into core system information. The technology supporting the work and learning will become more transparent to the user, rather than a distraction from the real goal. A richer social learning ethos will encourage networks of practice to spring up where previously, isolated pockets of similar disciplines reinvented various forms of the wheel. The online environment is unique in its ability to support collaboration and the building of information structures we haven't thought of yet.

Glossary

Alignment   Arrangement of elements on a page along an implied line to form visual connections

Alphanumeric   Mix of letters and numbers

Ascender   The part of a letter that reaches up into the space between lines of text: b, d, f, h, l, t have ascenders

Back matter   Items following the body text of a document or book, such as appendices, bibliography, glossary

Balance   A stable state in which opposing forces cancel each other

Bleed   Graphics or illustrations (rarely print) are sometimes printed to the edge of the paper, giving a "bleed" edge

Bibliography	List of publications consulted by the author of a document
Boldface	A heavier, darker version of the body type in use
Breadcrumb list	A navigation list that shows the full path from the home page to current page
Bullet	Dot or mark used to emphasize items in a list
Callout	Words next to a figure, describing it, connected by a line
Caption	Explanation accompanying an illustration or visual element
Composition	Combination of elements which form a whole
Consistency	Agreement between components that repeat throughout a document
Controlled vocabulary	Use of a specified list of terms for searching subjects
Copyfitting	Adjustments made to text copy to permit it to fit into the layout space available
Counter	The space inside of a closed portion of a letter, such as O, A, B, P
Crop	Removal of a portion of a photograph

Descender	The part of a letter that reaches down into the space between lines of text: g, j, p, q, y have descenders
Document	(n) Printed page or pages forming a logical whole
Downstyle	Use of initial capital letter only in a phrase or heading
Duplex printing	Printing on both sides of the paper
E-learning	Technology supported learning, usually Internet-based
Em dash	Long dash between words—signifies a break in thought in a sentence
En dash	Short dash between words—used between words that indicate a range, such as "20–30"
Flush and hung	First line is flush to the margin and subsequent lines are indented
Flush left or right	Set with the left or right margin even or justified
Focal point	The part of a composition most emphasized
Folio	Page number
Font	Complete collection of one size of a given style of type

Front matter	Pages preceding the body of a book or document, such as foreword or table of contents
Glance box	A box containing highlighted information on a page; designed to be read at a glance
Grid	Predefined format for layout
Gutter	Can refer to the binding edge of a page or the white space between columns of text
Header	Information found at the top of each page
Hypertext/ Hyperlink	Usually underlined, this text links to related information
Information design	Practice of making information easy to find, understand, and remember
Inverted pyramid	Organization of content starting with the main point and going on to supporting points and further detail
Italics	Slanted type resembling handwriting
Job aid	Performance support tool describing steps and decisions a jobholder should follow
Justified type	Even alignment of type, also called flush
Kerning	Altering the spacing between selected pairs of letters
Landscape	Lengthwise page orientation

Layout   Arrangement of items on a page, document, Web site, etc.

Leading   White space between lines of type

Legibility   Speed with which words can be recognized—type design is a determinant

Link-rot   Change in Web links that occurs when sites they are connected to are removed

Military specifications   MIL-SPEC is a structured format for documents produced for the military, or in this manner

Naming conventions   A standard pattern of limited vocabulary to ensure consistency throughout a document

Orphan   A short word or syllable occupying a line at the end of a paragraph; copyfitting adjustments should be made to clear the copy of orphans

Pagination   Process of putting page numbers into place

Pica   Printer's measure equal to 0.166 inch—there are about 6 picas to the inch

Point   The measurement of type size. One point is equal to 0.0139 inch. There are 12 points to the pica and about 72 points to the inch.

Portrait	Page orientation in which shorter ends form top and bottom
Ragged type	Opposite of justified type, in which lines of type form an uneven margin
Readability	Ease of reading a printed page—type arrangement is a determinant
Repository (knowledge)	An organized, shared storage space for educational content
Rules	Lines used to set off elements on a page
Sans serif	Type without finishing strokes, such as Arial
Saturation	The intensity of a color
Serif	Type with added finishing strokes, such as Times Roman
Simplex printing	Printing on one side, the right side, of the paper
Storyboard	A series of cartoon-like panels depicting a sequence of descriptive scenes with illustration and text
Symmetry	Opposite halves of a combination in balanced arrangement
Template	In software, a generic program that can be customized

Typeface All the type of a single design, such as Times Roman

Type family All the styles available based on one basic design, for example: Lucida is available as condensed, bold, expanded, and blackletter

Web safe color 216 Web safe colors display as solid ("non-dithered") on any computer monitor or Web browser

Widow A line of isolated text from a preceding paragraph forced to the next page; copyfitting adjustments should be made to clear the copy of widows

Wizard Not the mythical character with magical powers! This is a feature in many software applications that allows you to create memos, newsletters, résumés, and slide presentations easily by establishing default settings or customizing settings in a step-by-step process.

X-height The height of the body of a lowercase letter is called the x-height. Ascenders reach above the body and descenders reach below it.

Reference List

Babbie, Earl. *Survey Research Methods*. Belmont, CA: Wadsworth Publishing Company, 1990.

Behrens, Roy R. *Design in the Visual Arts*. Englewood Cliffs, NJ: Prentice Hall, Inc., 1984.

Book, Albert C. and C. Dennis Schick. *Fundamentals of Copy & Layout: A Manual for Advertising Copy & Layout*. Chicago: Crain Books, 1984.

Bringhurst, Robert. *The Elements of Typographic Style*. Point Roberts, WA: Hartley and Marks, 1992.

Collins, Mauri P. and Zane L. Berge. "Technological Minimalism in Distance Education." *The Technology Source,* November/ December 2000.

Flanders, Vincent and Michael Willis. *Web Pages That Suck: Learn Good Design by Looking at Bad Design*. San Francisco: Sybex, 1998.

Fleming, Jennifer. *Web Navigation: Designing the User Experience*. Sebastopol, CA: O'Reilly, 1998.

Gagné, Robert. *Essentials of Learning for Instruction.* Englewood Cliffs, NJ: Prentice Hall, 1988.

Gedney, Karen and Patrick Fultz. *The Complete Guide to Creating Successful Brochures.* Brentwood, NY: Asher-Gallant Press, 1988.

Genesee Survey Services, Rochester, NY. *www.gensurvey.com*

Hodges, John C. and Mary E. Whitten. *Harbrace College Handbook.* NY: Harcourt, Brace & World, Inc., 1967.

Hurlburt, A. Layout: *The Design of the Printed Page.* NY: Watson-Guptill, 1977.

International Paper Company. *Pocket Pal.* NY, 1974.

Jordan, Lewis. *The New York Times Manual of Style and Usage.* NY: Times Books, 1976.

Kushner, Malcolm. *Successful Presentations for Dummies.* Foster City, CA: IDG Books, 1997.

Mager, Robert F. *Making Instruction Work, or Skillbloomers.* Belmont, CA: Lake Publishing Company, 1988.

Meggs, Philip B. *Type and Image: The Language of Graphic Design.* NY: Van Nostrand Reinhold, 1989.

Meyer, Eric K. *Designing Infographics: Theory, Creative Techniques, and Practical Solutions.* Indianapolis: Hayden Books, 1997.

Mok, Clement. *Designing Business: Multiple Media, Multiple Disciplines.* San Jose, CA: Adobe Press, 1996.

Newby, Timothy J. and Donald A. Stepich. "Designing Instruction: Practical Strategies." *Performance & Instruction,* August–December 1989.

Raines, Claire, and Linda Williamson. *Using Visual Aids: A Guide for Effective Presentations.* Menlo Park, CA: Crisp Publications, Inc., 1995.

Rand, Paul. *From Lascaux to Brooklyn.* New Haven: Yale University Press, 1996. (anything by Rand!)

Spiekermann, Erik, and E. M. Ginger. *Stop Stealing Sheep and Find Out How Type Works.* Mountain View, CA: Adobe Press, 1993.

Sternberg, Harry. Composition: *The Anatomy of Picture Making.* NY: Pitman Publishing Company, 1958.

Strunk, W., and E. B. White. *The Elements of Style,* 3rd ed. NY: Macmillan, 1979.

Tufte, Edward R. *Envisioning Information.* Cheshire, CT: Graphics Press, 1990. (any book by Tufte!)

White, Jan V. *Graphic Design for the Electronic Age.* NY: Watson-Guptil, 1988.

Wickiser, Ralph L. *An Introduction to Art Education.* NY: World Book Company, 1957.

Wilson, Adrian. *The Design of Books.* Salt Lake City: Peregrine Smith, 1974.

Wong, Wucius. *Principles of Two-Dimensional Design.* NY: Van Nostrand Reinhold, 1972.

Wurman, Richard Saul. *Information Architects.* NY: Graphis, Inc., 1997.

Xerox Corporation. *Xerox Publishing Standards*: *A Manual of Style and Design.* NY: Xerox Press-Watson Guptill, 1988.

Zinsser, William K. *On Writing Well: An Informal Guide to Writing Nonfiction.* 4th ed. NY: Harper Collins, 1990.

Index

Active voice.. 30
Alignment.. 40, 128, 299
Ascender... 62, 83, 299
Balance.. 45, 299
Binding.. 125, 129, 130-131
Body text............... 54, 64, 79, 84, 88, 115, 225, 244
Boldface.................................... 69, 70, 143, 225, 300
Boxes... 73, 74, 147
Brochure........................ 75, 79, 110-111, 116, 167, 174
Builds.. 244, 251
Business cards... 116-118
Capital letters... 89-90
Charts... 149-160
    bar chart......................... 150, 152, 154, 155
    fever chart.. 154
    flow chart.................................. 159-160, 222
    pie chart..................................... 155-157
    schematic diagram......................... 157-158
Coherence.. 46

Color.. 91-106
    choice... 101, 106
    connotations... 101-104
    depth.. 93, 94, 103
    hue... 95
    intensity... 93, 94, 254
    schemes... 95-98
    shade... 94
    temperature.. 93
    value... 93-94
Compliments slip.....................................119, 175
Composition............................... 40, 42-43, 45, 49
Contrast....................................... 39, 46, 53, 70
Copyfitting................................... 66, 180, 300
Copyright................................... 122, 245
Cover.....................................110, 127-128
Cropping.....................................137-139
Descender....................................62, 300
Diagram................................... 161-162
Discussion area................................ 293
Document map................................. 193-194
Document sequence................................ 121
Dominance................................... 47
Downstyle.......................... 64, 90, 147, 301
Emphasis.............................. 47, 69, 70-71
Flipchart............................... 263-265
Flowchart.......................... 159-160, 222
Focal point................................ 76, 301
Font................................... 83-88
Forms................................... 199-210
Frames................................... 279
Gagné, Robert...................11, 12, 13, 32, 307
Graphics................................... 133-144
Graphs................................... 149-152
Grid.................... 55, 180, 284, 286, 287, 302
Handout................................... 237-239
Heading................................ 54, 84, 191-194

Identity.. 113-114
Interaction... 275-276
Invoices... 118
Italics... 69
Job aids.. 219-222
    cheat sheets... 219
    check list.. 221
    decision table.................................. 220, 222
    decision tree................................... 222, 288
    flow chart....................................... 158-160
    matrix............................... 34, 146-148
    procedure............................ 159, 217, 221
    worksheet... 220
Justification.. 59
Kerning............................. 62-63, 278, 302
Keystone effect... 246
Knowledge repository......................... 293-297
Landscape orientation.................................. 117
Layout....................................... 71-82, 302
Learning management system....................... 294
Learning outcomes... 13
Legibility.................... 59, 64, 69, 89-90, 303
Letterhead... 113-116
Line.. 41-42
Line length................................. 61, 88, 277
Links.................................. 269, 280-281
List.. 35, 255
Mager, Robert................... 7, 8, 19, 218, 234, 308
Maintenance... 285
Manuals.. 88, 191
Margin..58-59, 80
Master slide........................241, 244, 255
Media decision.. 239
Menu.................... 173, 205, 270-271, 288-289
Metaphor................................ 33-34, 93, 269
Meyer, Eric K.................. 135, 149, 150, 153, 308
Navigation................... 33, 49, 53, 63, 67, 272-275, 279

Negative space... 42, 44, 70
Newsletters.. 177-184
Notification.. 294
Objectives... 19-22
Organizing information... 23
Outline view.. 191-193
Overhead projector... 243-247
Page number.. 60
Pagination.. 65, 303
Paper... 109-111
Paragraph.. 29, 55, 59, 65
Passive voice... 30
Portrait orientation.. 117, 244
Positive space.. 42
Postcards... 175-176
Posters... 211-215
Presentation checklist... 239
Presentation software.. 250, 253-257
Progressive disclosure... 246
Proportion.. 47
Proximity... 47, 204
Readability... 28-31, 69-70, 303
Readings.. 152, 154, 293
Repetition.. 15, 49, 53, 77
Reports... 191-198
Résumés... 223-229
Rhythm.. 49
Rule lines.. 73-74, 210
Rule of thirds.. 138
Runaround... 59, 64
Search... 278-279
Self-mailer... 69
Sentence spacing... 63
Shape... 40, 43, 47, 76, 77, 84, 85, 89, 94, 246
Site map.. 274, 280
Size... 43
Slides.. 249-251

Spreadsheets..185-189
Stationery..113-120
Storyboard.........................235-236, 273-274, 276, 304
Style..67-68, 191-194, 241
Style sheet...67, 241, 244
Subheading...48, 55, 63
Survey..206-210
Symbol...32-33, 42
Tables...145-148, 284
Target audience..........................7-10, 75, 169, 236
Templates..194, 255, 304
Texture..44, 76, 95
Translation..178, 260
Tufte, Edward...............105, 106, 133, 144, 145, 149, 272, 283, 309
Typeface...83-90
    combining...84
    sans serif...............................83-87, 278, 304
    serif......................................83-87, 278, 304
Unity...49, 72, 77, 106
Version control..197
Video...259-262
Wall charts...217-218
White space...............................44, 117, 244, 264
Wurman, Richard Saul...............................5, 23, 309
Xerox Publishing Standards.................28, 29, 80, 88, 309

ABOUT THE AUTHOR

Christine Sevilla, MPA, MS, founded her business, *luminguild,* in 1997 to focus on helping people to do their jobs better. She leads seminars on information design, conducts courses and focus groups on the Web, and creates instructional systems, both online and traditional, for a varied array of clients. She and her husband, Timothy Wells, have coauthored many articles. She also serves as adjunct faculty for the Rochester Institute of Technology, teaching online graduate courses.

Would you like to discuss aspects of this book with the author or with other readers? Join the discussion at luminguild.com/infodesign.

Other Books in Design & Creativity from Crisp

Rapid Viz
Kurt Hanks and Larry Belliston
An introduction to the methods of capturing visual details without formal
art or design training.
1-56052-055-8

Wake Up Your Creative Genius
Kurt Hanks and Jay Parry
An invigorating course in creativity that can turn bright ideas into success.
1-56052-111-2

The Universal Traveler
Don Koberg and Jim Bagnell
The classic book on problem-solving techniques that can be used in almost
any discipline or career from art to creative writing.
1-56052-045-0

Rousing Creativity
Floyd Hurt
A very accessible approach to creativity that transforms concepts into
actions using techniques and group processes that produce results almost
immediately.
1-56052-547-9

Experiential Drawing
Robert Dvorak
The simplest introduction possible to the techniques of sketching and
drawing for people who want to express themselves visually.
1-56052-065-5

**Available at bookstores everywhere or from Crisp at
CrispLearning.com**